GLOSTER
JAVELIN

GLOSTER JAVELIN

AN OPERATIONAL HISTORY

MICHAEL NAPIER

Pen & Sword
AVIATION

First published in 2015 by
Pen and Sword Aviation

An imprint of
Pen & Sword Books Ltd
47 Church Street
Barnsley
South Yorkshire
S70 2AS

Copyright Michael John William Napier © 2015

ISBN 9781473848818

Editor: Jasper Spencer-Smith
Design and artwork: Nigel Pell
Proof reader: Martin Derry

Printed and bound in Malta
By Gutenberg Press Ltd.

Pen & Sword Books Ltd incorporates the Imprints of
Pen & Sword Aviation, Pen & Sword Family History, Pen & Sword Maritime,
Pen & Sword Military, Pen & Sword Discovery, Pen and Sword Fiction,
Pen and Sword History, Wharncliffe Local History, Wharncliffe True Crime,
Wharncliffe Transport, Pen & Sword Select, Pen & Sword Military Classics,
Leo Cooper, The Praetorian Press, Seaforth Publishing and Frontline Publishing

For a complete list of Pen & Sword titles please contact
PEN & SWORD BOOKS LIMITED
47 Church Street, Barnsley, South Yorkshire, S70 2AS, England
E-mail: enquiries@pen-and-sword.co.uk
Website: www.pen-and-sword.co.uk

Contents

FOREWORD

by
Air Marshal Sir F. B. Sowrey, KCB, CBE, AFC

Officer Commanding, 46 Squadron
Javelin FAW 2, 1958-1960

This book about the Javelin is based on the experiences of those who operated it, both in the air and on the ground. The author's own background as a 'fast jet' pilot in the Royal Air Force gives him a unique insight into the flying characteristics of the aircraft and the part it played at the leading edge of development of tactics for the higher-performance fighters that followed.

In the 1950s, the operational need was for a high-performance fighter that could intercept incoming raids by day or night, in all weathers and under conditions of massive jamming of air-defence radars. Supersonic (in a very steep dive) and fitted with an effective air-intercept radar, the Javelin met this requirement admirably. Through the late 1950s and into the early 1960s, the Javelin formed the frontline of our air defences, and with successive improvement, ultimately it became the first aircraft in RAF service to be missile armed. Later, the ability to make long-range overseas deployments was greatly enhanced by the fitting of an air-refuelling probe on the Javelin – the first RAF fighter to have this capability – which acted not only as a distance improver but also a 'force multiplier.'

Flying the Javelin fostered a close working understanding between pilot and nav/rad to achieve the best results. That experience was to lay the foundations of the crew cooperation that was needed to operate the more sophisticated two-seat aircraft that followed, such as Phantom, Buccaneer and Tornado. The crews who operated the Javelin showed the highest levels of professional competence – they were ready able and willing to fight if necessary and they played their part in showing the West's determination to deter aggression during the 'Cold War.'

Freddie Sowrey

INTRODUCTION & ACKNOWLEDGEMENTS

Often overlooked by aviation historians and enthusiasts alike in favour of its more 'glamorous' single-seat contemporaries, the Gloster Javelin was a remarkable aircraft which occupies a unique place in the post-war history of the RAF. It was the first complex fast-jet aeroplane to enter service with the RAF: a high performance two-engined, two-crew, radar-equipped fighter, the service's first aeroplane to have been designed from the very outset to be a night/all-weather fighter, the first front-line type to be armed with air-to-air missiles and the first of the RAF's tactical aircraft to be capable of routine air-to-air refuelling. I hope that by describing the work of Javelin squadrons through the late 1950s and early 1960s my book will restore the Gloster Javelin to its rightful place in the operational history of the RAF and that in future, aviation historians will give the type the recognition it truly deserves as one of the pivotal types operated by the service.

Although this is an operational history of a remarkable aircraft, it is more properly the operational history of the remarkable men who flew and serviced the Javelin. That story could not have been told without the active support of a number of 'Javelin Veterans' who have encouraged me – with great modesty and humour – to tell their story. They have helped me to do so by sharing their recollections and answering my questions, often with great patience. Although their number is quite small, they represent a good cross section of aircrew and groundcrew, from squadron commanders to junior first-tourists, senior officers to NCO aircrew, from engine technicians to instrument fitters. I am deeply indebted to the following 'Javelin Men' without whose generous support I could not have completed this book: Malcolm Adamson (85 Sqn), Brian Bullock (141, 41, 11, 25 and 29 Sqns), Jack Broughton (89, 85, 11 Sqns), Richard Carrey (87 Sqn), Peter Day (60 Sqn), Ed Durham (85 Sqn), Trevor Evans (64 Sqn), Roy Evans (25, 11 Sqns), Keith Fitchew (5, 64, 60 Sqns), Don Headley (64 Sqn), Sir Richard Johns (64 Sqn), Peter Masterman (29 Sqn), Mike Miller (JMTU, 23, 60 Sqns), Forbes Pearson (85, 29 Sqns), John Roberts (85 Sqn), Sir Freddie Sowrey (46 Sqn), Roy Smith (23, 11 Sqns), Gordon Wheeler (FCIRS, 85 Sqn), Alan Wright (46 Sqn).

I am very grateful to Judy Abell who kindly loaned her late husband John's log-book and superb 35mm slides to me and to Judy Cowper who generously gave me full access to her late husband Chris' extensive photograph collection and also loaned his log-book to me. Thank-you, too, to Alison Donovan for her kindness in lending me her late husband CJ's photographs, and arranging – via son Chris – access to CJ's log-book. This was particularly poignant for me, as CJ was my navigator on Tornado GR1s some 25 years after he flew Javelins.

I have tried to illustrate this book with 'operational' photographs – that is images showing aircrew and groundcrew doing their job, rather than simply those of static aircraft at air shows. Many of the photographs have not been previously published and I am extremely grateful to the following who have helped me in my research: Richard Gardner (FAST), Mike Smith (Newark Air Museum), Peter Elliott, Ian Alder, Belinda Day (all RAF Museum), Lee Barton (Air Historical Branch), Tim Kershaw (Jet Age Museum, Gloucester) – all of whom have helped me to find suitable photographs. Also many thanks to Tony O'Toole for his ever enthusiastic support and for sharing his collection of Javelin photographs. I am particularly indebted to Graham Pitchfork for his great help and support not only for introducing me to his Javelin contacts, but also for access to his own collection of photographs.

Another invaluable source of material has been the crew-room diaries of the current RAF squadrons that once flew Javelins. I am very grateful to the following squadron members who made me welcome in those crew rooms: Simon Devenish (3 Sqn), Andy Paul (5 Sqn), James Pearce (11 Sqn), Richard Watts (29 Sqn), Steve Mills (33 Sqn), Steve Beardmore (41 Sqn), and Nick Graham (72 Sqn) (via e-mail).

Thanks are due to the following fellow writers and researchers: Tom Docherty (72 Sqn Historian), Roger Lindsay (whose work on individual aircraft histories has been a great help) and Guy Ellis (who generously shared his research on the Zambia detachment in 1966).

I'm grateful to Pete West for his superb artwork and also to my son Tom for his ideas for the book jacket. Finally, I am grateful beyond words to my editor Jasper Spencer-Smith who originally had the idea for this book and whose enthusiasm for books and for all things aviation and military is both infectious and inspiring.

one

ENTRY INTO SERVICE
1952 – 1957

Exercise *Beware*

Noon on 23 September 1955 marked the start of one of the largest air-defence exercises held in the United Kingdom (UK) since the end of the Second World War. Code named Exercise *Beware*, the week-long operations pitted the country's day and night fighters against large raids by 'enemy' aircraft provided by RAF Bomber Command, the USAF and 2 Tactical Air Force (2 TAF). Although the day-fighter force, newly-equipped with the Hawker Hunter, proved reasonably effective against attacking English Electric Canberras, Vickers Valiants and North American B-45 Tornados, it was clear that the de Havilland Venom and Armstrong-Whitworth Meteor night fighters were outclassed by the latest generation of high-performance bombers. Indeed, in his post-exercise report on *Beware*, Air Marshal Sir Dermot Boyle, KCVO, KBE, CB, AFC, noted that 'the lack of a modern night fighter was a palpable weakness' in RAF Fighter Command. However, *Beware* was also the operational debut of a new all-weather fighter, which promised to take back the advantage from the bombers: the Gloster Javelin. Two Javelins (FAW 1s, XA554 and XA559) operated by the All Weather Fighter Development Squadron (AWFDS) flew from RAF Coltishall and, in the words of *Flight* magazine: 'acquitted themselves admirably.' By the end of the exercise, one of the Javelins, flown by Wg Cdr E. D. Crew, DSO★, DFC,★ and his navigator/radar operator (nav/rad) Sqn Ldr J.H. Walton, had eight Canberra silhouettes painted on its nose, evidence of a busy and very successful week.

The successes by Crew and Walton were a welcome vindication of the new aircraft. Only two months earlier, the *Sunday Express* had run a front-page story under the headline 'New Fighter Shock' in which it stated that the Javelin 'is displaying serious defects and, in its present form, could never be put into front-line service.' The article also alleged

The Operational Readiness Platform (ORP) at RAF Coltishall during Exercise Beware, *September 1955. The two Javelins operated by the All Weather Fighter Development Squadron (AWFDS) are at the far end of a line-up of de Havilland Venom NF 3s from 141 Squadron.*

that the Javelin exhibited; 'undesirable and sometimes alarming' characteristics at high speed and that it suffered from a 'mysterious vice' which had caused the crashes of three prototypes. Sir Frank Spriggs, managing director of the Hawker-Siddeley Group, had quickly dismissed the article as 'pure tripe' and pointed out that the safety record of the Javelin was comparable to that of other British and US-built high-speed aircraft. However, it was true that development of the aircraft had not gone entirely smoothly – but perhaps that was not surprising for what was a radical new design.

GA 5 Development

The Javelin had started life in the late 1940s as the Gloster GA 5, in response to a Ministry of Supply (MoS) specification F4/48 for a high-performance night and all-weather fighter. After receiving proposals, the MoS ordered the building of two prototype aircraft: the GA 5 and the de Havilland DH 110. The types offered two very different solutions to the various challenges posed by the specification. De Havilland had opted for a swept-wing aeroplane, which owed its twin-tail boom configuration to its lineage through the Vampire and Venom. Ultimately, the DH 110 was not selected by the RAF, but was developed for the Royal Navy as the Sea Vixen all-weather fighter for the Fleet Air Arm (FAA). Meanwhile the Gloster Aircraft Company, under the leadership of their chief designer R.I. Walker, FRAeS, chose a distinctive delta-wing configuration which combined the best stability and control characteristics at high subsonic speeds within a simple and robust structure. In a departure from 'conventional'

The tailed-delta configuration chosen by the Gloster design team is clearly visible as the third prototype Gloster GA5 (WT827) banks over south Gloucestershire. The type was cleared to 535kt at low level: above 35,000ft it was (theoretically) supersonic – but in practice a steep dive would be required to reach the limit of 1.04M. (G. R. Pitchfork)

delta designs, the Gloster team included a tail plane. This latter innovation enabled them to add trailing-edge flaps to the wings, thus ensuring a nose-low attitude on final approach, to make landing easier in poor visibility.

On 26 November 1951, the prototype GA 5 (WD804) was flown for the first time by Sqn Ldr W.A. Waterton, AFC★, Gloster's chief test pilot, at RAF Moreton Valence near Gloucester. The maiden flight was not without incident: in his book, *The Quick and the Dead: the Perils of Post-War Test Flying*, Waterton wrote that 'buffeting and banging set in somewhere around the tail end. At 200mph the whole airframe shook violently; a matter which afforded me considerable concern.'

The vibration problem was soon resolved and flight development trials progressed reasonably well over the next seven months, until this aircraft was destroyed in an accident. On 29 June 1952, the elevators broke off the aircraft during a high-speed run, leaving Sqn Ldr Waterton with no direct pitch control; instead of abandoning the aircraft, he managed, in an exceptional piece of flying, to land the aircraft at Boscombe Down. Unfortunately, the aircraft broke up on landing and caught fire. After freeing himself from under his jammed canopy, Waterton re-entered the burning fuselage to retrieve the flight-data recordings. For his courage during this episode, Waterton was awarded the George Medal (GM). Despite this setback, and Waterton's criticism of the aircraft's control forces, the development flying had gone well enough and the GA 5 was ordered into quantity production in July 1952. The following month it was officially christened the 'Javelin'.

The fourth prototype (FAW 1, WT830) was almost lost when, on 4 March 1953, Sqn Ldr J.A. Sowrey, DFC, experienced a failure of the powered-aileron controls. Once again the test pilot chose not to abandon the aircraft and, in another piece of exemplary flying, Sowrey managed to land the aircraft safely. However, the next two Javelin accidents, both of which involved low-speed handling trials, were fatal: Lt P.G. Lawrence, MBE, was killed on 11 June 1953 after entering a deep stall and Flt Lt R.J. Ross was killed on 21 October 1954, when he was unable to recover from an intentional spin. Another Javelin crashed during spinning trials on 8 December 1955, but on this occasion Sqn Ldr A.D. Dick was able to eject from the aircraft successfully.

Although a question mark always remained over the low-speed handling characteristics of the Javelin, the aircraft was, in reality, no worse in that respect than later generation fast-jet aircraft: no squadron pilot would, for example, dream of intentionally stalling a Phantom, a Jaguar or a Tornado. Moreover, the Javelin was fitted with a stall-warning system, which, along with light buffeting from the wings, gave the pilot ample warning that he had reached the limiting angle of attack. But pilots who were used to being able to stall or spin an aircraft at will, were slow to adapt to the concept of not being able to do so. Also they were unimpressed by the fact that performing a loop – a very basic aerobatic manoeuvre – was specifically prohibited in the Javelin. In fact the Javelin could be looped successfully, but the restriction reflected the mechanics of the elevator artificial-feel system: at low speed the system introduced a nose-down pitch, which would act in the wrong sense if the aircraft was inverted at the top of a loop. To overcome this, the pilot would have to pull much harder against the force of the elevator artificial-feel system, but this quirk was considered to be an unacceptable handling risk.

The RAF Night-Fighter Force

Fighter Command's night-fighter tactics of the mid-1950s were based on a chain of Ground Controlled Intercept (GCI) radar stations, sited at strategic points around the coast of the UK. These were served by a night-fighter force comprising eleven squadrons of what could best be described as 'interim' types. The de Havilland Venom NF 2/2A and NF 3 and the Armstrong-Whitworth Meteor NF 11 to NF 14 were all developments of single-seat day fighters, rather than aircraft designed specifically from the drawing board for the night-fighter role. Although the performance of the Venom and Meteor night fighters marked an improvement over the previous generation of piston-engined types, it still fell short of that enjoyed by the jet-engined bombers of the RAF. Nor could they match the performance of the latest Soviet bombers such as the Tupolev Tu-16 (reporting name Badger) or Tu-20/Tu-95 (reporting name Bear).

When enemy air activity was expected, night fighters would be brought to cockpit readiness on the Operational Readiness Platform (ORP), a purpose-built area next to the runway threshold. Once an incoming enemy raid was detected, the GCI controller would scramble the night fighters to make the intercept: fighters were vectored towards their target by the GCI controller until they could find it on their own on-board radar. In both the Venom and Meteor the heart of the weapons system was the US-manufactured Hughes AN/APQ 43 Airborne Interception (AI) radar (AI Mk.21 in RAF service), which had a useful range of approximately 14 to 18 miles for a Canberra-sized target. Once the target was displayed on the aircraft's radar, the nav/rad took over from the GCI controller to give the pilot instructions to complete the interception and engage the target with cannon. The system was often exercised and it worked well, but its 'Achilles Heel' was undoubtedly the poor performance of the night-fighter aircraft.

46 Squadron

January 1956, was very much the start of a new era for 46 Squadron, the resident night-fighter unit at RAF Odiham. At the beginning of January, the squadron commander Wg Cdr F.E.W. Birchfield, OBE, AFC, along with Flt Lt R. Franks, Sqn Ldr D.F.C. Ross and Fg Off D. Shaw were detached to Boscombe Down for 14 days to convert onto the Javelin FAW 1. Their first Javelin (FAW 1, XA570) arrived at Odiham at the beginning of February and the squadron's Meteor NF 11 and NF 14s were ferried to RAF Church Fenton for transfer to 72 Squadron.

As more aircraft arrived at Odiham, the crews started their conversion on to the new type. Staff from Boscombe Down continued to support the conversion process by providing briefings on the handling characteristics of the Javelin; navigator/radar operators (nav/rads) were also detached to Boscombe Down to familiarize themselves with the British-built Airborne Interception (AI) Mk.17 radar fitted to the Javelin FAW 1. Although the AI Mk.17 was broadly similar in performance to the AI Mk.21 that most navigators were used to, the two systems displayed the information in very different ways. The AI Mk.21 used a Plan Position Indicator (PPI) screen which gave a 'god's eye view,' whereas the AI Mk.17 employed a 'B' scope for range and angle off and a 'C' scope for range and elevation, which added considerably to the workload of the nav/rad when making an interception.

By May, fifteen Javelins had been delivered to 46 Squadron and despite the CO complaining that their serviceability rate was 'appallingly low,' all of the squadron's pilots had completed their conversion to type by the end of the month. Conversion of the nav/rads was continuing apace. Most pilots found the Javelin straightforward to fly and the only problems encountered were with close control by GCI above 40,000ft. These tactical problems, largely caused by the wider turning circle of the larger and faster Javelin, would be resolved over the next few months as crews and GCI controllers gained experience with the new type. Unfortunately the squadron lost its first Javelin (FAW 1, XA570), on 12 June 1956, when Wg Cdr Birchfield and Fg Off B. Chambers crashed on the approach to Odiham; both crew members were killed.

An intensive flying trial started the following month and continued into September. The trial, which involved eight aircraft, was intended to give the aircraft a good 'shake down' by flying 60 hours per month per aircraft until a total of 1,000 flying hours had been achieved. This involved flying almost continuously from dawn to dusk each day, the most noticeable effect of which was a huge increase in the workload of the groundcrew as they struggled to keep the aircraft serviceable. An over-night shift was introduced to cope with the burden and an extra rectification team was also attached to the squadron from August. To start with, most of the sorties flown during the trial comprised Practice Intercepts (PIs), starting initially at 30,000ft and progressing, as crews gained more experience with the aircraft, to 45,000ft. Towards the end of the trial period the first air-to-air firing sorties were flown. Unfortunately, these did not go very well: the nav/rads found it difficult to lock the radar onto the target to give accurate ranging information

Two Javelin FAW 1s from 46 Squadron at medium level. Note the slightly cranked wing leading edges and the distinctive 'pen nib'-type fairing around the jet pipes: a feature of production aircraft. During August and September 1956, the squadron carried out an 'intensive flying trial' involving 60hrs per aircraft per month. (RAF Museum)

to the pilots' gunsights and not many hits were scored amongst over 20,000 rounds that were fired in the first week's shoot. The problem was that rather than locking onto the target banner, the radar tended to lock onto the towing aircraft instead. This snag was initially overcome very simply by doubling the length of the tow-rope, which resulted in an immediate improvement in gunnery scores. Later, a more refined solution involved attaching a radar reflector onto the banner. Night air-to-air firing was also carried out at high-level to the south of the Isle of Wight, under the control of the Ventnor GCI station. Crews reported 'a brilliant flash from all four wing-mounted cannon' but their night vision was seriously impaired afterwards.

September 1956 also saw Exercise *Stronghold*, the nickname for that year's annual Fighter Command exercise. Although 46 Squadron was not officially participating in the exercise, two Javelins were diverted from the intensive flying trial during the first night phase and claimed a remarkable five kills in a ten-minute period. By early October the trial had been successfully completed and the Javelins participated fully in their first exercise, Exercise *Beaverbrook*, on 19 October. The first scramble was at 04:55hrs and six Javelins each intercepted USAF Douglas B-66 Destroyers between 24,000 and 40,000ft. There was a more challenging interception profile later in the month when Javelins were scrambled against Hunters flying at .85Mach (M) at 45,000ft. Unsurprisingly it proved much more difficult to intercept such small, high-flying, high-speed targets, but nevertheless all of the Javelin crews claimed successes.

In the aftermath of the intensive flying trial, Javelin serviceability was not good and typically, the daily serviceability was down to only a quarter of the sixteen aircraft on strength. The end of the year saw 46 Squadron crews consolidating their skill, while the

Javelin (XA623) 'G' of 46 Squadron over the Solent (Ryde pier is in the background) photographed, from the rear doors of a Blackburn Beverley from 47 Squadron, during a sortie for Flight magazine on 2 July 1956. The gun ports for the 30mm Aden cannon are visible on the leading edge of the wing. (RAF Museum)

beginning of 1957 brought a number of detachments to other Fighter Command airfields so that they could participate in more exercises. Exercise *Bomex*, a monthly exercise, which pitted Javelins against V-bombers at altitudes above 40,000ft for the first time. Operating at night firstly out of Church Fenton and then RAF West Malling in January, the Javelins of 46 Squadron claimed kills against Valiants and Canberras. On the night of 28 February, six Javelins launched from Odiham to intercept eight Valiants flying at 48,000ft: all the Valiants were claimed as kills.

The clean lines of early Javelins are evident in this view of Javelin FAW 1 (XA620) 'E' from 46 Squadron. Operating at high altitude, the Javelins were able to intercept V-bombers and Canberras far more successfully than had the previous generation of Meteors and Venoms. The squadron distinctive marking of a red arrowhead on a white bar is painted on the tail. (RAF Museum)

*Javelin FAW 1 (XA628) was initially issued to 46 Squadron, but like most of the unit's Javelin FAW1s, this aircraft was passed to 87 Squadron at RAF Brüggen, in late 1957, when 46 Squadron re-equipped with the FAW 2 variant. (*Newark Air Museum)

As well as PIs and air-to-air gunnery, the squadron's routine flying also included ciné exercises, where one aircraft would track another through a series of manoeuvres. March brought a reminder of the Javelin's unforgiving nature at slow speed when Flt Lt P.C. Gifkins spun from a mishandled ciné attack at 25,000ft; luckily he was able to recover the aircraft at 15,000ft.

Javelin Mobile Training Unit (JMTU)

While 46 Squadron was putting their Javelins through their paces in early 1957, the Venom night-fighter squadrons were preparing to exchange their aircraft for Javelins. Traditionally, the conversion process to a new aircraft was carried out 'in house.' Squadron pilots would read the Pilot's Notes for the new type and then collect the aircraft from the factory or Maintenance Unit (MU); after flying a few sorties to familiarize themselves with the new machine they would be declared operational once more. Although 46 Squadron had converted to the Javelin in much this way, it was clear that a complex aircraft like the Javelin demanded a more formal conversion process. In early 1957, a dual-control version of the Javelin was still two years away and although 228 Operational Conversion Unit (OCU) would start running Javelin conversion courses from RAF Leeming later in the year, there were still eight more front-line Venom and Meteor squadrons waiting to be re-equipped with Javelins during 1957 and 1958. Clearly it would be impractical for all these night-fighter crews to be cycled through a full OCU course, so an alternative arrangement was needed. The solution was the formation of the Javelin Mobile Training Unit (JMTU) under the command of former 46 Squadron Javelin pilot Sqn Ldr P.D.C. Street, DSC. The JMTU comprised two Javelin pilots, four navigators, two Valetta pilots and a sixteen-man groundcrew. It had no Javelins of its own, but it did have two Vickers Valetta aircraft. Of these, one provided the JMTU with its mobility, while the other one, equipped with an AI Mk.17 in the nose, was fitted as a 'flying classroom' for training the nav/rads.

The JMTU would arrive at the converting squadron's home base and run a two-week ground school. It would provide a Javelin 'cockpit simulator' – in reality simply a mock-up cockpit, which was used as a procedures trainer for pilots – and an AI Mk.17 caravan which contained a ground training rig for nav/rads. The JMTU staff, supported by representatives from the Gloster Aircraft Company Limited (to describe the airframe), Martin Baker Aircraft Limited (to describe the Mk. 3J ejection seats) and Armstrong Siddeley Limited (to describe the Sa.6 Sapphire engines), would deliver a series of lectures about the Javelin and its systems. The JMTU pilots would then collect the new aircraft from Moreton Valence or from the MU and deliver them to the squadron. Converting squadron pilots were given three sessions in the cockpit simulator before having a familiarization flight in the back seat of a Javelin flown by a JMTU pilot. They would then fly six day sorties and one night sortie before being considered 'operational on type.' Nav/rads were required to fly thirteen AI training sorties in the Javelin before becoming operational.

First Impressions

For experienced Meteor or Venom crews the first impression of a Javelin was its sheer size: at 56ft long it dwarfed the Venom, and weighing over 30,000lb, it was one-and-

By the standards of the day, the front cockpit of a Javelin was roomy, well laid out and ergonomically designed. This is a Javelin FAW 6, possibly XA831, which was used for research at RAE Farnborough. The cockpit of the Javelin was virtually identical throughout the various marks of the aircraft. (FAST Archive)

The cockpit of Javelin FAW 1 (XA622), the aircraft was used for instrument trials at RAE Farnborough. The 'traditional' flight instruments have been replaced by 'strip'-type Air Speed Indicator (ASI) and 'roller blind' Attitude Indicator (AI) which were used in the Gnat, Lightning and Buccaneer. (FAST Archive)

a-half times heavier than a Meteor. The two Sapphires provided the Javelin with twice the power of a Meteor, or three times that of the Venom. Both cockpits were roomy and well-laid out by the standards of the day. For pilots, the 'standard instrument panel' was familiar and the Javelin proved to be a relatively easy aircraft to fly on instruments. The main challenge was taxying the aircraft: it was equipped with – and steered – by hydraulic toe-brakes, which took some getting used to.

Once airborne the aircraft's powered controls were quite responsive and the aircraft compared favourably with other contemporary types. And, despite Sqn Ldr Waterton's earlier objections, front-line pilots did not find the control forces to be noticeably heavy. However, the most impressive features of the Javelin's performance were the short time that it took to climb to height (for example a Javelin FAW 1 took just eleven minutes to reach 45,000ft) and its ability to plummet almost vertically back down again without accelerating, thanks to the extremely powerful airbrakes. This latter characteristic enabled crews to remain on task until they reached a very low fuel state and then to recover to overhead base at a very economical high-level cruise, before descending into the circuit with minimal fuel burn for recovery. Flt Lt R.A.R. Carrey,

The airbrakes (seen fully extended) on the Javelin were powerful and effective. They were operated by means of a small lever located between the throttles and could be selected to any position between fully retracted and fully extended. (FAST Archive)

who had flown the Hunter and the Supermarine Swift noted, 'the official ceiling of 48,000ft was easily achievable. Lack of a pressure-breathing jerkin prevented the ceiling being higher, but we did practice interceptions at 50,000ft without trouble.'

The Groundcrew View

A typical Javelin squadron would have some 120 groundcrew, which included expertise in all the various trades required to keep the aircraft serviceable. 'Most of us at technician rank had undertaken specialist courses,' recalled Cpl J.A. Roberts who served on 85 Squadron, 'in my case the aircraft fuel system and an engine course at Bristol Aircraft at Filton... The groundcrew were organized with most of the manpower split into two shifts – 'days' from 08:00hrs (normally) until late afternoon (nominally 17:00hrs) manning the day flying programme plus any ongoing rectification tasks, and 'nights' from 16:30hrs and manning the night-flying programme and rectification to generate the required aircraft for next days' programme. [In addition] there was a small day deep maintenance team progressing routine servicing and 'deep' rectifications.' Another 85 Squadron member, instrument fitter Cpl G.R. Wheeler, continued, 'the day shift handled a wave in the morning and a wave in the afternoon, each wave consisted of about eight aircraft with a duration of about two hours. The night shift was about the same finishing about 05:00hrs with the aircraft refuelled, turned round and covered up. The beauty of night shift was that it started Monday evening and finished on Friday morning so it gave one a long weekend. Of course this did not happen during AOC inspections, if there was an exercise or if the squadron was on QRA.'

Javelin groundcrew enjoyed something of a 'love-hate' relationship with the aircraft as Cpl Wheeler describes, 'although flight crews liked the Javelin it was a pig of an

A groundcrew carrying out a turn-around at night on a Javelin FAW 4. Unfortunately the ergonomic care that had gone into the cockpit was not evident in the accessibility of aircraft systems for servicing and maintenance: the groundcrews often had to work in confined and awkward spaces.

A 'liney' [line engineer] uses a wheel chock as an improvised step to reach into the engine starter bay. The cartridge-starter system used a twin-breech firing mechanism and three spare cartridges stored in the servicing bay. In the foreground, starting cartridges lie on the concrete.

A Javelin FAW 4 of 141 Squadron being worked on by the groundcrew. On a night/all-weather squadron, much of the work had to be done in the dark and outside – regardless of weather. Flying often continued long into the early hours of the morning which meant maintenance teams were kept busy throughout the night.

aircraft to service. Unlike the Hunter, were some thought had gone into accessing components, the Javelin designers did not put any thought into it at all. A few examples are: firstly, the jet pipe temperature amplifier, which was out of sight of an access panel the opening of which was just big enough to get it out with juggling. Secondly, the yaw damper components in about 18-in square compartment where each item was clipped in, but the clips could not stand the vibration so we landed up parcelling them up with locking wire - not a pleasant job in such a confined space. Thirdly the fuel contents sensors, which were always going u/s with water contamination, required the tank units to be changed, which required the removal of panels with about eighty screws. Finally, the radio and radar section was the biggest on the squadron because after each sortie the radar system needed some form of attention.'

This opinion was echoed by Jnr Tech T. Evans, who served on 64 Squadron and felt that, 'the Javelin was not easy aircraft to work on from the airframe fitter's viewpoint. Most of our work involved gaining access to the hydraulic systems via a panel situated on the underside of the aircraft. Here were the three hydraulic reservoirs, flap and airbrake pre-selector valves and just about everything else. The problem was that the manuals illustrated this conglomeration of pipes and valves looking inboard with the engine intakes removed. We of course were looking outboard so everything was back-to-front. This also meant that most of the hydraulic pipes were in front of the valves. With the flap and airbrake pre-selector valves being identical we had to be quite careful the first few times these had to be changed. The rigging of these valves in conjunction with the selector valves to achieve a smooth and synchronized deployment of the flaps and airbrakes was a long and reiterative process. Dare I admit that wire locking the air-pressurization pipe to the union on number three reservoir (at the top of the bay and almost out of sight) was very much a hit and miss affair. The radio antenna sited in front and to the left of this access bay was the culprit for many a scar on the left shoulder blade… almost a rite of passage for a Javelin airframe fitter.'

A Javelin FAW 4 painted with the black and white leopard's head markings of 141 Squadron. This mark of Javelin was fitted with improved flying controls including an all-flying tail plane and a row of vortex generators ahead of the ailerons. (RAF Museum)

141 & 23 Squadrons

It is perhaps an illustration of the immaturity of the design of the Javelin that nine different marks of the aircraft were introduced into service within the space of just four years. Furthermore, the second mark of the aircraft to enter operational service was not the FAW 2 but the FAW 4. In the latest mark, Gloster had introduced some refinements to the flying controls: the elevators were replaced by an 'all-flying tail' for pitch control, while roll control was improved by a row of vortex generators fitted just ahead of the ailerons. Fuel capacity was also increased by the fitting of two 250-gallon external ventral tanks, which became the standard fit on most Javelins. The aircraft entered service in February 1957 with 141 Squadron, which was temporarily based at RAF Horsham St Faith (near Norwich) while the runway at Coltishall was resurfaced. The JMTU arrived at Horsham St Faith the end of January, followed a week later by first two Javelin FAW 4s; by the end of March the squadron had fourteen Javelins on strength. The work-up continued through the next two months while the JMTU moved across the airfield to run conversion of 23 Squadron, also on to the FAW 4. On 19 May, 141 Squadron was declared operational with the Javelin, just in time to participate in Exercise *Vigilant*.

Exercise *Vigilant*

Following from *Beware* and *Stronghold* in the previous two years, *Vigilant* was Fighter Command's annual air-defence exercise of 1957. It differed slightly in format from its predecessors in that enemy raids were concentrated into specific

Javelins from 23 Squadron perform a mass start-up at RAF Coltishall before a flypast over the presentation parade for the squadron's standard by Marshal of the Air Force Sir John Slessor, GCB, DSO, MC on 28 June 1957.

periods (two daytime and one night time) each day, rather than spaced randomly throughout the whole exercise period, so that long hours were not wasted on periods of unproductive 'standby.' It was also the first time that a significant Javelin force was integrated into Fighter Command's order of battle. At short notice, 46 Squadron deployed the eight crews of 'B' Flight to Leeming for the exercise, a move completed within twelve hours. During three nights of operations 'B' Flight claimed fifteen kills against Valiants and Canberras, but they felt that the Northern Sector did not make full use of the Javelins for long-range interceptions. This the crews found 'most frustrating.' Back at Odiham 'A' Flight were launched against day and night raids and made claims against an impressive variety of types including Dassault Mystère IV, Douglas A-3 Skywarrior, Fairey Gannet AS 4, North American F-100 Super Sabre and Boeing B-47 Stratojet.

For the Javelin wing at Horsham St Faith, the exercise got off to an exciting but almost disastrous start. One of the ventral tanks of a 23 Squadron aircraft became partially detached while it was taxying out to the ORP. The tank scraped along the taxiway and eventually the fuel ignited. The Javelin crew only became aware of the conflagration underneath their aircraft when the air traffic controller called to them 'you're on fire.' Unfortunately two Hunter pilots also heard the call and thought that it applied to them, which resulted in the loss of two Hunters. The Javelin pilot, Flt Lt J. Wilkinson, and his navigator evacuated their aircraft over the nose and Wilkinson was reported to have received slight injuries to his feet as a result of 'landing on the tarmac in a running position.' The Javelin burnt out completely, but mercifully the fire did not extend to a line of nearby 141 Squadron aircraft. For the rest of the exercise, the aircrews of both 23 and 141 Squadrons were kept

The Javelin aircrew serving on 46 Squadron in late 1956 or early 1957; in the background is a Javelin FAW 1. The squadron were often deployed to other bases for exercises such as RAF Church Fenton (January 1957), RAF Duxford (February 1957) and RAF Wattisham (March 1957). (RAF Museum)

busy; the groundcrews were hard-worked too, servicing the aircraft in a biting 30kt wind blowing off the North Sea. *Flight* magazine reported excitedly, 'in the last phase of the exercise a Vulcan was intercepted at 50,000ft over the North Sea by one of the Javelins.' Fighter Command's own more measured report recorded that, 'overall results achieved at night by the Javelins were more than three times better than those of the Meteor and Venom night/all-weather fighters also participating.'

151 Squadron

A third Venom squadron started its conversion – to a third mark of Javelin – in June 1957. That month the JMTU pilots delivered the first Javelin FAW 5s to 151 Squadron, which had temporarily moved to RAF Turnhouse (Edinburgh) while the runway at RAF Leuchars was resurfaced. This latest version of the Javelin differed from the others by having additional internal fuel tanks in the wings. The operational range of the early Javelins had been limited because of their inadequate fuel capacity and although the ventral tanks went some way to rectifying the problem, the increased fuel load of the FAW 5 – equivalent to an extra ventral tank – was still much needed. For their part, the pilots of 151 Squadron were 'unanimous in their praise for the handling qualities of the Javelin, which is a beautiful aircraft to fly… indeed flying a Javelin after the Venom is like driving a Bentley after an MG.'

Javelin FAW 5 (XA661) 'Z' of 151 Squadron flies past the Bell Rock lighthouse. The squadron's blue and white St Andrews Cross marking is visible on the tail. During the squadron's conversion to the Javelin it operated from RAF Turnhouse (Edinburgh) while the runway at RAF Leuchars was resurfaced.

228 Operational Conversion Unit (OCU)

Although the work of the JMTU was far from complete, 228 OCU started receiving its own Javelin FAW 5s in June, so that it could start training new crews on the aircraft. All of these pilots and nav/rads had already completed at least one tour on other fighter types. The four-month course introduced crews to flying the Javelin and then concentrated on honing their skills at PIs. By August, all the advanced squadrons on the OCU had completed their own Javelin conversion.

August 1957 was also the month that 46 Squadron were re-equipped for a second time, this time with the Javelin FAW 2. This model was essentially similar to the FAW 4 except that it was equipped with the US-built Westinghouse AN/APQ-43 (AI Mk.22) radar, which was broadly the same AN/APQ that had been fitted in the Meteor and Venom. Unfortunately the new airframe/radar fit suffered from teething

An echelon of Javelin FAW 1s from 46 Squadron photographed during the summer of 1957, just before they were replaced with FAW 2s. The squadron carried out several flypasts in the summer of 1957 including one at RAF Leuchars for HM the Queen. (Jet Age Museum)

Two newly-delivered Javelin FAW 2s on 46 Squadron get airborne in formation (note the revised squadron markings on the tail fins) This version was equipped with the US-built Westinghouse AN/APQ-43 (AI Mk.22) radar, similar to that fitted in the night-fighter Meteor and Venom. (RAF Museum)

Javelin FAW 4 (XA757), from 141 Squadron, about to land RAF Geilenkirchen, Germany on 12 September 1957 to take part in Exercise Counterpunch. *In the two weeks the squadron operated from there it carried out seventy-seven 'scrambles' during the exercise and claimed 103 'kills' against Canberras, F-84F Thunderjets, Meteors and Valiants.*

From late 1957, most Javelins were fitted with ventral tanks. These are clearly visible on Javelin FAW 5 (XA715) 'T' from 151 Squadron as it taxies along the runway. Each tank had a capacity of 250 gallons: the two tanks contained enough fuel for up to an extra 30 minutes flying time. (Philip Jarrett)

problems and for the first few months there were some problems in the serviceability of the AI Mk.22. The squadron's surplus Javelin FAW 1s were transferred to re-equip 87 Squadron at RAF Brüggen, which became the first Javelin unit in RAF Germany.

The SBAC show at Farnborough in the first week of September 1957 was an opportunity for Britain's aircraft manufacturers to show off their latest products and, on the five days that the weather permitted, there was an impressive flypast

Javelin FAW 5 (XA717) 'V' of 151 Squadron takes off for a practice sortie. The FAW 5 variant benefitted from having an increased internal fuel capacity (approximately another 250 gallons) over the earlier marks of the aircraft. In September 1957, the squadron deployed to RNoAF Sola (near Stavanger) for Exercise Strikeback.

Javelin FAW 5 (XA661) 'Z' of 151 Squadron, crewed by Flt Lt Burrows and Fg Off Hamilton, ran off the runway after a hydraulic failure on landing at RAF Leuchars in November 1957. The aircraft was repaired but later caught fire while on the strength of 11 Squadron at RAF Geilenkirchen on 29 October 1962. (RAF Museum)

by a formation of 27 Javelins from 46, 23 and 141 Squadrons and 228 OCU. Then at the end of the second week of September both 141 and 23 Squadrons deployed to Germany to take part in the NATO Exercise *Counterpunch*. Twelve Javelins from 141 Squadron flew from RAF Geilenkirchen during the exercise, while twelve Javelins from 23 Squadron operated from RAF Ahlhorn. The fighters were scrambled to intercept targets including Canberras, Republic F-84G Thunderjets, Meteors, B-45s and Valiants at long range, typically some 100 to 150 miles away from base. However, 46 Squadron had a quiet time of *Counterpunch*, largely because poor weather curtailed flying from Odiham.

Meanwhile, hastened by the promise of a deployment to Norway for Exercise *Strikeback*, a major NATO naval operation, if they were ready in time, 151 Squadron crews continued their conversion to the Javelin. The incentive worked and eight Javelins duly deployed to the Royal Norwegian Air Force (RNoAF) base at Sola on 16 September. During the exercise, 151 Squadron acted as targets for FAA fighters, mainly from the aircraft carrier HMS *Ark Royal* (RO9). Taking the place of 151 Squadron at Turnhouse, 46 Squadron enjoyed a more successful time with Exercise *Strikeback* than they had with *Counterpunch*, managing a high success rate, despite the problems associated with their new radar. On one night Sqn Ldr H.G. James and Fg Off I.M. Calder made a successful interception 200 miles from base.

The shorter nose of the AI Mk. 22-equipped Javelin is apparent on this Javelin FAW 6 (XA815) 'E' of 89 Squadron. Also visible are the two rows of vortex generators – one just ahead of the ailerons, the other just behind the wing leading edge The squadron markings comprise a dark blue stripe on a light blue bar. (W.M. Adamson)

89 & 29 Squadrons

The rolling programme of re-equipment for night fighter units continued in September when the last of the Venom NF 3 squadrons, 89 Squadron, based at RAF Waterbeach, exchanged their aircraft for yet another mark of Javelin – the FAW 6. Just as the FAW 2 differed from the FAW 4 in its radar fit, so the FAW 6 differed from the identical FAW 5 airframe by being fitted with the AI Mk.22. In the operations diary, Flt Lt A.J. Prosser wrote that 89 Squadron's pilots, 'expressed their delight at the aircraft's handling qualities and the well laid out cockpits. How pleasant it is to fly an aircraft in the role for which it was primarily designed, instead of a mutilated version of a mundane day fighter.'

Two months later, the first of the Meteor NF 14 units, 29 Squadron, started its conversion to the Javelin FAW 6 at RAF Acklington. Although the first flight of a 29 Squadron Javelin took place in November, the slow delivery rate of aircraft meant that the squadron would not be operational with the new type until June 1958.

two

EARLY YEARS
1958 – 1959

Routine

By the beginning of 1958 Fighter Command's Javelin squadrons were well settled into night/all-weather fighter operations. An 89 Squadron nav/rad, Flt Lt J. Broughton, recalled that 'the routine established on an RAF night/all-weather fighter squadron was that one flight flew during daylight hours and the other checked in on Monday for a night-flying test (NFT) and then flew during the darkness nightly through to and including Thursday. Training comprised exercises and practice interception, ciné, gunnery, and cross-country flights. Aircraft normally flew as a pair or on occasion in battle formation of fours. Of course the various sector and command exercises and Quick Reaction Alert (QRA) exercises interrupted this cycle.' Each month there were routine day-long exercises such as *Bomex*, *Ciano* and *Kingpin-Adex* in which fighters were scrambled to intercept targets provided either by Bomber Command or Fighter Command. Exercise *Ciano* also frequently included Electronic Countermeasures (ECM) training, either jamming or chaff, which the GCI and fighters had to work through. In the case of radar jamming, the ARI 18006 Torist equipment fitted to the AI radar allowed the aircraft to home onto the jamming source.

A rather more tedious duty was the inaccurately named Exercise *Fabulous*, which became Exercise *Halyard* in 1958, and which involved keeping two armed aircraft at cockpit readiness in case intruders were detected in UK airspace. Each fighter squadron took a week's turn at maintaining readiness from the ORP at Waterbeach; the Hunter squadrons would cover the daylight hours while the Javelin squadrons covered the nights. *Fabulous/Halyard* was an extremely unpopular duty with squadron commanders, who saw the loss of a week's flying as a major threat

Javelin FAW 6 (XH696) 'H' of 89 Squadron fitted with ventral tanks. The squadron, which was declared operational in December 1957, was called for Exercise Halyard *at very short notice in the last week of January 1958. (W.M. Adamson)*

to their ability to meet their monthly flying hours' target. Neither did the air – and ground – crews relish the thought of a week of enforced idleness. 'The most boring duty was cockpit readiness,' wrote Sgt W.M. Adamson, a nav/rad on 89 Squadron. According to Fg Off F.M. Pearson, a nav/rad on 85 Squadron, 'the flight on night duty held six crews apart from flying: two crews sat in the crew room on thirty minutes readiness. Two crews sat with them at ten minutes, readiness but fully kitted up… 'Mae West' on and 'bone dome' to hand… and two crews sat in the cockpit of two aircraft parked out on the end of the runway on the ORP at two minutes

Javelin FAW 6 (XA800) 'L' of 89 Squadron at RAF Stradishall, this aircraft was written-off when the undercarriage collapsed on landing at the airfield on 2 February 1958: the crew, Flt Lt B.R. Kent and Fg Off M.J. Fairey escaped unhurt. (W.M. Adamson)

readiness. The crews at cockpit readiness wore flying suits… no immersion suits in those days. The groundcrew passed up blankets and cups of tea as the cockpits were unheated and had to remain open regardless of the weather to prevent the canopy misting up. We were connected by telebrief to the GCI who played endless LPs of Frank Sinatra and others to keep us awake with occasional weather and diversion updates. After ninety minutes we all moved up one slot and the crews in the cockpit came back to the crew room to start at thirty minutes readiness. We did this routine all night and after a few nights QRA – back and forth to the runway in winter weather it got very cold.' It was no less unpleasant for the groundcrew: Cpl G.R. Wheeler, of 85 Squadron, pointed out that, 'it was very cold during the winter and Norfolk is well known for its lazy wind… it went through you instead of going round you.'

In the words of Wg Cdr F.B. Sowrey, OC 46 Squadron, the mainstay of Javelin flying was, 'lots and lots and lots of instrument flying and flying at night… the primary role of a night/all weather was to be prepared to operate in conditions which were not altogether comfortable. You might go off not being certain that you're going to be able to get back to your base.' To be able to operate effectively in marginal conditions, pilots had to be both confident and capable at flying on instruments. And once in the operating area, the tactical focus of routine flying was on PIs. 'Lashings and lashings and lashings of PIs,' continued Sowrey, '… it was training for the crews, but don't forget that it was also training for the GCI controllers.'

Apart from PIs, the other regularly practised events on Javelin squadrons were ciné weave and air-to-air gunnery. For ciné, 'the target aircraft entered a descending turn at about forty-five degrees of bank, allowing the attacker to close up and start tracking,' recalled Flt Lt R.A.J. Carrey (a pilot on 87 Squadron). 'The target then did a barrel reversal into a climbing turn the other way. The attacker had to start filming at exactly six hundred yards, closing to exactly two hundred yards before

46 Squadron Javelin FAW 2 XA814/O on the line at West Raynham during the Squadron Commanders' All Weather Fighter Leaders Course, June 1959. In the same month Wg Cdr Sowrey led his squadron to victory in the Ingpen Trophy. Note that the first two aircraft sport different versions of the squadron markings. (F.B. Sowrey)

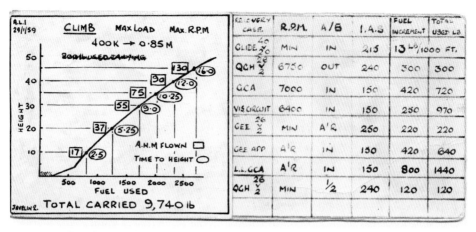

A 46 Squadron 'get you home' card for the Javelin FAW 2 – a cockpit aide-memoire giving the fuel burn for various climb and descent profiles. This enabled crews to determine how long they could remain 'on task' before recovering to base. (F.B. Sowrey)

making a spot reversal. Both ranging and tracking were very strictly marked, and there were heavy penalties if the opening and closing ranges were not precise.' Points were scored by counting the number of film frames in which the gunsight 'pipper' was within a certain distance of the target's cockpit. While ciné was relatively straightforward and pilots could achieve satisfyingly high scores (Carrey himself achieved 97 percent), gunnery was something of a black art.

Javelin Gunnery

Air-to-air gunnery was practised against a 30-ft long banner, which was towed on a long cable by a tug aircraft. The cannon shells were dipped in paint so that they would leave a coloured trace around any holes they made in the flag; each aircraft was loaded with ammunition of one colour, so that each pilot's scores were uniquely marked. When 46 Squadron started air-to-air firing in September 1956 the results had been quite low, at around 5 percent. Over the summer of 1957 when 141 Squadron started air-to-air firing too, they achieved disappointing scores. For example, in June their average score was just 1.8 percent. This was considerably less than they might have expected to achieve, with scores around 15 percent being the order of the day for a typical day fighter squadron. The discrepancy was largely due to the fact that the Javelin's cannon were wing- rather than fuselage-mounted, as on the Hunter, Meteor and Venom day fighters. Fuselage-mounted guns were much closer to the sight line and also delivered a tighter concentration of fire than wing-mounted guns. As Flt Lt Carrey explained, 'It was important to have as concentrated a bullet pattern as possible at the normal firing range. When firing at a flag target, this was two hundred to two hundred and fifty yards. With the inner guns about twenty feet apart, this meant toeing each gun about a degree inwards,

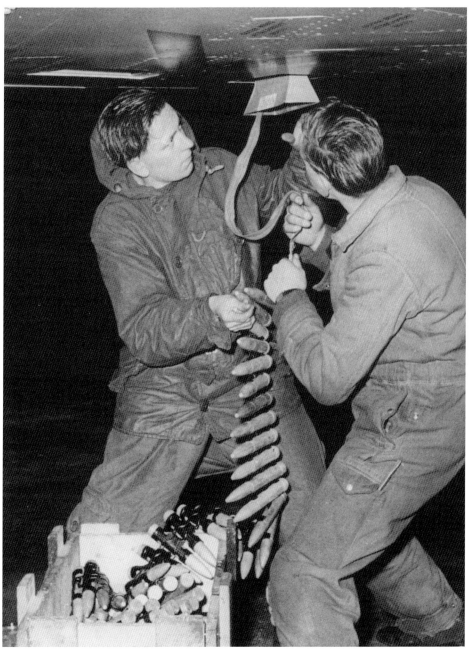

LAC Cooper and Cpl Lynch re-arming the 30mm Aden cannon armament of a Javelin FAW 4 in service with 141 Squadron. After the guns had been fired at night, re-arming was carried out during an Operational Turn Round (OTR) in which the aircraft was replenished as quickly as possible. At first this took around 30 minutes, but was halved when groundcrews became more familiar with the aircraft.

Javelin FAW 6 (XA822) 'G' of 29 Squadron, on final approach; with full flap selected the approach speed would typically be around 130kt. The first Javelin for the squadron arrived at RAF Acklington on 31 October 1957 and the unit was declared operational on 1 June 1958. (W. Grundy via G.R. Pitchfork)

and rather more for the outers. This does not sound much, but it makes firing at exactly the right range more critical. All APC firing was done with the inner guns, as the outers did not have sufficient scope for adjustment. For operational use the guns were harmonized at two hundred and fifty yards (inners) and four hundred yards (outers). There was also the suspicion that the wings flexed enough under load to upset the harmonization, which was our excuse for not getting as high scores as the day fighters.'

Another complication was that of radar ranging: being able to judge the correct amount of deflection to aim ahead of the target depended on knowing the range very accurately. If the radar did not work, or gave erroneous readings, the gunnery accuracy suffered. Both 23 Squadron (in March 1958) and 29 Squadron (in September 1958) reported that they had found 'obscure electrical problems' in the gunsight ranging; however solving these problems did not appear to alter the scores noticeably. Only 151 Squadron, which carried out harmonization of its aircraft, cannon and radars in April 1958, achieved any appreciable accuracy and they were able to score a squadron average consistently of around 11 percent. For most Javelin units, the average score for air-to-air gunnery was around 7 to 9 percent.

That said, individual scores could be remarkably high, particularly amongst the Pilot Attack Instructors (PAIs): in August 1959, Flt Lt V.L. Hill and Flt Lt G. Roberts of 29 Squadron scored 32 percent and 37 percent respectively, while Fg Off L.G. Buckingham of 23 Squadron had managed 38 percent the previous summer. However, the highest individual score was a remarkable 44 percent achieved by Flt Lt D.W.S. Stedman (of 151 Squadron) in April 1958. As OC 29 Squadron, Wg Cdr

The cartridge-starter system used on the Armstrong Siddeley Sapphire engine caused a spectacular amount of smoke as the cartridges fired – and start-up fires were not unusual. The aircraft is a Javelin FAW 5 of 151 Squadron.

A.R. Gordon-Cumming, wrote succinctly, there was, 'no black magic about getting good scores on the Javelin, but that as usual practice makes perfect.'

41 Squadron

A series of squadron disbandments, at the beginning of 1958, saw the re-numbering of 141 Squadron to become 41 Squadron, following the demise of the Hunter day-fighter unit with that number, which had been based at Biggin Hill. The beginning of the year also saw two serious flying accidents. The first one, to a 23 Squadron aircraft (FAW 4, XA734), occurred shortly after take-off on 11 February and was caused by a catastrophic failure of the starboard engine; the fuselage caught fire, burning away the tail and causing structural failure. The crew ejected successfully, but the immediate result for the Javelin force was the introduction of temporary restrictions to the Sapphire engines, which in turn caused some limitations to the aircraft's operational performance. Unfortunately the second accident, which occurred two weeks later, was a fatal one. Both crew were killed when the pilot was inadvertently ejected from a Javelin (FAW 7, XH714) operated by the Aircraft and Armament Experimental Establishment (A&AEE). This highlighted the unreliability of the system of latches designed to secure the Mark 3J ejection seat into the aircraft under conditions of negative-g and sadly it was not be the last such accident.

The restrictions on Sapphire engines, which lasted until the early summer,

A Javelin FAW 4 of the 'new' 41 Squadron in formation with a Hawker Hunter F 6 of the 'old' 41 Squadron in February 1958. There was a major shuffling of squadron numbers to preserve the existence of 'senior' units as the RAF was reduced in the aftermath of the 'notorious' 1957 Defence White Paper. (41 Squadron)

effectively restricted useful PIs to around 41,000ft. Some squadrons also removed the ventral tanks from their aircraft to compensate by reducing weight and drag while the restrictions were in force. However, routine training continued unabated. Short detachments to RAF stations in Germany became a regular feature of the flying programme and, for example, Brüggen was visited by 46 Squadron in March 1958, 151 Squadron in April and both 23 and 41 Squadrons in May. In the first week of June, 46 Squadron also visited Brüggen to take part in the NATO Exercise *Full Play*, during which it operated from the ORP as part of an integrated Javelin wing with the resident 87 Squadron. The engine restrictions caused some frustration amongst the crews, not least because late launches by GCI were exacerbated by the increased time to 40,000ft (18min from the usual 12min), making it difficult sometimes to intercept incoming raids in time. Meanwhile, 89 Squadron, which had detached to RAF Ahlhorn for the exercise, flew a large number of successful scrambles. The squadron further reported that it had been, 'impressed by the general indifference of 2 TAF to weather minima.' Other Javelin squadrons had also participated in *Full Play* from the UK: the newly-operational 29 Squadron fielded four aircraft and 41 and 151 Squadrons also took part, the latter having detached to Waterbeach for the exercise.

Routine flying was not without its hazards, whether they be technical or operational. On 6 March, Flt Lt J. Sneddon and Flt Lt J. Broughton had an alarming incident over London (FAW 6, XA820). 'Jock Sneddon and I took off singly for some continuation training at 18:30hrs. By the time (8 to 10min) we got to 35,000ft over the Thames Estuary it was just getting dark when there was a loud bang, the aircraft rolled inverted and we were looking up at the Thames. It transpired the hood had come off its rail on one side and peeled off hitting the fin about half way up. Jock quickly brought the aircraft under control and we set off for base. The main problem was because of the blast we couldn't communicate with each other apart from the occasional shouting contest and it was cold.'

A rather more serious incident occurred on 14 April, when a pair of 46 Squadron aircraft collided during a night PI. The starboard side of the tail plane on Flt Lt T.F. Carter's aircraft (FAW 2, XA805) was removed and the fin buckled as it sliced through the port wing of Flt Lt E.P. Marsh's Javelin (FAW 2, XA809). Both aircraft remained flyable and both landed safely. It is a remarkable testament to the skills of Javelin crews that such collisions were very rare, given that PIs regularly involved closing in on an unlit target for a visual identification at night.

A formation of Javelin FAW 5s from 151 Squadron flying at low-level: The second aircraft carries the markings of 29 Squadron, which suggests this was taken during practice for the flypast at the Farnborough Air Show in September 1958.

Two Javelin FAW 7s from 33 Squadron get airborne for a training exercise. The squadron received its first aircraft at RAF Leeming in June 1958 and became operational four months later and was moved to RAF Middleton St George. The aircraft typically operated in pairs, taking it turns to act as fighter and target. (33 Squadron)

33 Squadron

On 1 June 1958, 29 Squadron was declared operational. After a short break in the activities of the JMTU, now under command of Sqn Ldr M.H. Miller and sometimes also referred to as the Javelin Mobile Conversion Unit (JMCU), the conversion of Meteor night-fighter units continued. Once again there was a new mark of Javelin, this time the Javelin FAW 7. The first unit to receive this version was 33 Squadron, who received their first aircraft in July 1958. The Javelin FAW 7 probably represented the standard of the aircraft that should have first entered service: it was equipped with the more powerful Sapphire Mk203/204 engines and retained most of the improved fuel capacity of the FAW 5 and 6; perhaps more importantly, it could be armed with air-to-air missiles. In fact the first aircraft delivered to the RAF did not yet have a missile capability, but the modification process was relatively straightforward.

Javelin FAW 7 (XH835) 'NP', was the personal aircraft of Wg Cdr N. Poole, the commanding officer of 33 Squadron. Like many FAW 7s, this aircraft was later modified to FAW 9 standard; it was later issued to 60 Squadron in Singapore. (33 Squadron)

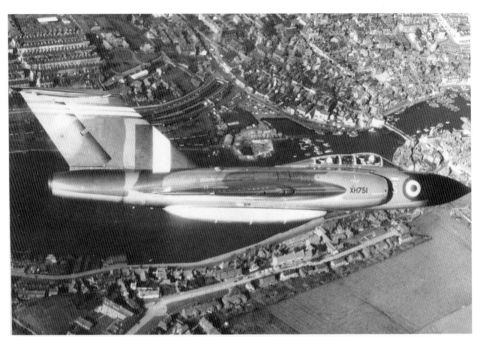

Javelin FAW 7 (XH751) 'S' of 33 Squadron banks over Whitby: The squadron markings comprise a red strip over a light blue band with dark blue edging. The revised layout of the jet-pipe fairing for the Sapphire Mk203/204 engine is visible. (33 Squadron)

The Javelin FAW 7 was the first mark of the aircraft to be capable of carrying Air-to-Air Missiles (AAM). Shown is XH756 armed with de Havilland Firestreak missiles, which was used for development work by the College of Aeronautics (CAe) before being passed to 23 Squadron. (Jet Age Museum)

Two Javelin FAW 7s of 33 Squadron take off from their home base at RAF Middleton St George [now Teesside airport]. The squadron spent most of the summer of 1958 converting to the Javelin and participated in Exercise Sunbeam, *soon after being declared operational.* (33 Squadron)

Summer 1958

The revolution in Iraq in mid-July overthrew the pro-western government and set the whole of the Middle East into turmoil. The crisis spread quickly to Lebanon and Jordan, where intervention by, respectively, US and British troops safeguarded the status quo. In response, all Javelin squadrons in Fighter Command were brought to one-hour readiness, with fully-armed aircraft, on 18 July. This state was maintained for a week, before being relaxed to a night-only

The view from one of the rear elements of the impressive formation of forty-five Javelins – led by Wg Cdr F.B. Sowrey, commanding officer of 46 Squadron, and made up from 46, 29, 89 and 151 Squadrons – which flew over the SBAC Air Show at Farnborough in September 1958. (RAF Museum)

An impressive spectacle: forty-five Javelins, led by Wg Cdr F.B. Sowrey, flying in formation over Farnborough. Sowrey had borrowed an Avro Anson in the previous few weeks to familiarize himself with the route – leading such a large and unwieldy formation was no mean feat of airmanship.

requirement for a handful of aircraft. These aircraft were eventually stood down on 6 August.

Aside from the summer's crisis in the Middle East, Sgt W.M. Adamson noted that, 'one item which stands out from my log book is how much formation practice we did… AOC's visit, Queen's birthday, Empire Games and SBAC flypasts.' Throughout the summer of 1958 (as in most years) RAF aircraft took part in a large number of flypasts: there was a flypast over London for the Queen's Birthday in May by a formation comprising 23, 41 and 89, as well as various flypasts to commemorate the Battle of Britain in September. However, the SBAC exhibiton, Farnborough, at the beginning of September, was a major commitment for virtually the entire Javelin force. As in the previous year, 46 Squadron were tasked to provide the lead. The challenge set for Wg Cdr Sowrey was to lead a mass formation of 45 Javelins and 45 Hunters over Farnborough on each of the display days. Steering such a large formation over exactly the right point on the ground at exactly the right time was no mean feat of airmanship and as Wg Cdr Sowrey later commented, 'no matter how hard you use modern technology, for the last bit you are down to the mark one eyeball.' The Javelins were provided by 46, 29, 89 and 151 Squadrons, much to the irritation of some of the squadron commanders who felt that the exercise provided very little training value in return for a massive commitment of their aircraft and manpower. However despite their objections, the large formation of Javelins and Hunters gave the crowds at Farnborough an impressive spectacle.

Cyprus

Earlier in 1958 the focus of short detachments had been Germany, but by October Fighter Command was looking further afield for its Javelin squadrons. In September 23 Squadron deployed to Cyprus to participate in Exercise *Dragon*. Five aircraft left

Javelin FAW 5 (XA667) in 41 Squadron colours of a red 'Cross of Lorraine' flanked by red and white bars. The squadron moved from RAF Coltishall to RAF Wattisham, where it arrived in 'Cross of Lorraine' formation. (41 Squadron)

A Javelin FAW 6 (XH696) 'H' from 89 Squadron at high level above the clouds: Although 'Pilots'Notes' for the type quoted a service ceiling of 48,000ft, crews found that in practice the Javelin could climb much higher with relative ease. (W.M. Adamson)

Four Javelin FAW 7s of 33 Squadron in echelon formation. With the extra power from the Sapphire Mk. 203/204 engines and unencumbered by drag from wing pylons and acquisition rounds, the gun-armed FAW 7 had the best performance of all marks of Javelin. (33 Squadron)

Horsham St Faith on 24 September, staging through Orange (France) and Practica de Mare (Rome) to RAF Luqa (Malta). The following day they continued to RAF Nicosia via a refuelling stop at RAF El Adem (Libya). Until the advent of air-to-air refuelling, Javelins would follow a similar route whenever they deployed from the UK to the Middle East. During Exercise *Dragon*, a local air-defence exercise which took place over the first three days of October, the Javelins flew PIs against Cyprus-based Hunters and Canberras.

Closer to home, Fighter Command's Javelin force, now comprising 23, 29, 33, 41, 46, 89 and 151 Squadrons, took part in the annual command exercise, code-named *Sunbeam*, which started on 16 October. The four-day exercise consisted of a morning afternoon and night phase each day, culminating in operations under simulated fall-out conditions that might be experienced in the aftermath of a nuclear exchange.

Sqn Ldr F.W. Sledmere, AFC, briefs crews of 151 Squadron at RAF Leuchars for Exercise Sunbeam *in October 1958. In the front row are, left to right: Sqn Ldr Tedder (commander 'A' flight), Sqn Ldr Maynard (nav/rad leader) and Fg Off Reed. Frederick Sledmere later commanded 5 Squadron, a Javelin unit, and was station commander at RAF Bawdsey.* (RAF Museum)

On final approach, Javelin FAW 7 (XH794) 'L' of 64 Squadron is about to land after a night sortie. The squadron tail markings of a blue scarab flanked by interlocking red and blue zig-zags are painted on a white bar. This aircraft served with 33 and then 5 Squadron after conversion to FAW 9 standard. (D.G. Headley)

Javelin FAW 7 (XH840) 'H' of 64 Squadron's makes a low overshoot at dusk; much of the flying on an all-weather fighter squadron was carried out at night. This aircraft was later destroyed in a refuelling accident at RAF Luqa (Malta) on 27 September 1961 while being ferried to 60 Squadron in Singapore. (D.G. Headley)

64, 25 & 85 Squadrons

The year closed with the conversion of two more Meteor squadrons to the Javelin FAW 7: 64 Squadron, which was normally based at RAF Duxford, moved temporarily to RAF Stradishall to start its conversion at in September and finally that year, the JMTU arrived at Waterbeach to convert 25 Squadron to its new aircraft type. A final adjustment to the Javelin squadron line-up was the re-numbering of 89 Squadron (also based at Stradishall) to become 85 Squadron at the beginning of December. By the New Year, 64 Squadron had completed its conversion and the unit had moved back to Duxford. By February 1959, the commanding officer of 25 Squadron, Wg Cdr K.H.H. Cook, DFC, recorded that, 'all pilots on the squadron strength have now completed several flights [in the Javelin] and without exception are most impressed with the aircraft's performance. Practically all pilots are now "sonic"'

The penultimate task of the JMTU was to help to convert 23 Squadron from the Javelin FAW 4 to the FAW 7, which was done in February 1959. It then moved to Church Fenton for 72 Squadron to convert on to the type. The first Javelins were delivered to Church Fenton in March and the JMTU arrived on 6 April. This was

Three generations of Gloster-designed fighters flown by 72 Squadron in formation on 11 June 1958. A Javelin FAW 4 (flown by Wg Cdr V.G. Owen-Jones, DFC) leads a Meteor NF 14 (Sqn Ldr I.P.W. Hawkins) and a Gladiator (Mr G. Worral). (72 Squadron)

The flight line at 85 Squadron: the unit was renumbered from 89 Squadron at RAF Stradishall in December 1958 (although this shows the squadron's Javelin FAW 8s at RAF West Raynham two years later). An English Electric Canberra T17 is visible at the extreme left.

to be the final duty of the JMTU, which disbanded once first the Javelin flights by 72 Squadron were completed. With 72 Squadron operational with the Javelin, all of the all-weather squadrons in Fighter Command were, at last, equipped with a truly capable fighter. Furthermore, and despite a debate amongst the Air Staff in 1957 which threatened to cancel the trainer variant of the Javelin, deliveries of the dual-control Javelin T3 started in March 1959. Initial deliveries were to 228 OCU, but during the course of the year each squadron also received its own 'trainer.' These aircraft were used for periodic checks on pilots and for instrument ratings (which up until then had been flown on the Meteor T 7), so for the first time pilots could be formally checked in their front-line type.

Light-Strike Role

Although the Javelin was primarily a high-level interceptor, trials began in 1959 of another, almost polar opposite, role. The question of how best to deal with the night-time threat from high-speed torpedo boats was being considered and 46 Squadron was chosen to participate in trials run by the Central Fighter Establishment (CFE) to assess the Javelin's potential as an torpedo-boat killer. Over the four weeks from 27 January, some squadron crews flew from Leeming to familiarize themselves with low-level operations. During this phase, they flew sorties against motor launches in the North Sea. The second phase commenced on 25 February and involved working with a Royal Navy destroyer and a Royal Netherlands Air Force (RNLAF) Lockheed P-2 Neptune, initially by day and later by night. The formal trial, Exercise *Halfback*, took place between 19 and 26 May and was flown from Stradishall. At the beginning of the month, crews practised low-level night PIs to get used to

A Javelin FAW 4 of 41 Squadron banks across an empty sky. In June 1959, the squadron carried out a simultaneous exchange of six aircraft and crews with 3 Squadron which had recently formed with FAW 4s at RAF Geilenkirchen. (41 Squadron)

the low-level environment again before *Halfback* started. The exercise itself involved carrying out low-level simulated strafe attacks against patrol boats at night, under the illumination of flares dropped by the controlling patrol aircraft. Flt Lt A.W.A. Wright, a 46 Squadron pilot, remembered that, 'we cruised out at about 2,000ft and we shut one engine down because at low-level the engines really drunk fuel… we were given a target fix from a Neptune or a Shackleton and the nav/rad would plot a steer towards it. As we got near to the nav's 'Gee' plot we relit the other engine so that we'd have both running for the attack… The nav would call out the heights as we attacked… it was a good way to hear the range of frequency of the nav's voice: it got higher and higher as the aircraft got lower and lower. It got quite exciting as we recovered from the attack as we went from a brightly lit sea through the flares and straight into a black velvet bag. It was all rather fun.' Despite poor weather, the Javelin crews managed some success, but this rather 'hairy' tactic was not subsequently adopted.

Overseas Detachments

Early 1959 saw the beginning of longer overseas detachments by Fighter Command's Javelin units. When 41 Squadron deployed to RAF Sylt for a two-week Armament Practice Camp (APC) in February. The venue for the annual APCs of the Germany-based RAF fighter squadrons in 2 TAF, Sylt was an ideal location for practising weaponry. Unfortunately for 41 Squadron, the weather was appalling for the entire fortnight they were there and the detachment was not a successful one. The following month it was the turn of 46 Squadron and they were blessed with fine weather. All pilots managed to fly nine live sorties on the flag. The only downside was the loss of a Javelin (FAW 2, XA802) which exploded and caught fire while starting up for the return flight home. Flt Lt M.E.O. Haggerty's aircraft burnt out, but amazingly a bottle of duty-free whisky, which had been loaded into the ammunition bay, survived the inferno intact.

Ranging slightly further afield, 33 Squadron deployed to Cyprus in mid-February. Flying from Nicosia, crews used the next fortnight for PIs and air-to-air gunnery, before participating in Exercise *Rickaby*. During this exercise, which ran for the first few days of March, 33 Squadron was charged with the night defence of Cyprus and claimed forty-seven kills against the attacking force of Canberras and Valiants.

Three Javelin squadrons also deployed to the continent to take part in the major NATO air-defence Exercise *Topweight*, which took place from 13 to 16 April. In fact *Topweight* involved all Javelin squadrons (less 46 Squadron which was holding readiness for Exercise *Halyard*), but while 23, 25, 41, 64 and 85 squadrons remained in the UK, 29 Squadron deployed to Øerland near Brekstad, Norway, while 33 and 151 Squadrons went to RAF Brüggen and Geilenkirchen respectively. The exercise started early on 13 April for the units based on the continent – and a steady flow of targets kept them busy for the next three days. Both air and groundcrews lived at the dispersals, working a shift system throughout the exercise. As well as numerous scrambles, aircrews spent nearly 40 hours at cockpit

On the pan at Nicosia, 5 March 1959: a 'scoreboard' showing forty-seven claims from the forty sorties flown by 33 Squadron during Exercise Rickaby is chalked on the nose of Javelin FAW 7 (XH835); the squadron's 'kills' included forty-five Canberras and two Valiants. (33 Squadron)

readiness. Meanwhile the UK-based squadrons enjoyed a more relaxed pace: during daylight hours they acted as simulated bomber targets for the continental squadrons. On one such sortie Sgt Adamson, of 85 Squadron, remembers: 'we flew in a line–abreast formation to Germany, simulating a bomber intrusion on a broad front. It was a clear day and we could see the Hunters of 2 TAF rising to intercept us. The Boss, centre man in the formation, got the extreme wingman to call when the Hunters were about to get into firing position. On the report, the Boss called for "airbrakes." Now if there was one thing the Javelin was good at, it was rapid deceleration. The Hunters shot past us, their firing solutions all to 'pot' and it was a simple task for our pilots to lower the nose and catch the Hunters in the gunsights, happy days.' At night, though, the UK-based Javelins reprised their role as fighters. These night sorties varied from those launched from the ORP and routine PI sorties, which had been adjusted to coincide with the expected timings of bomber raids. The targets intercepted ranged from V-bombers (including Handley Page Victors flying fast at 0.9M, at an altitude of between

A formation of 33 Squadron's Javelin FAW 7s seen over Athens harbour. The Squadron spent the whole of October in Cyprus and eight of the squadron's aircraft deployed to Larissa from Nicosia on 30 October 1959. (33 Squadron)

Short finals: a 33 Squadron Javelin about to touch down at the Royal Hellenic Air Force base Larissa during the goodwill visit to Greece during the first week of November 1959. (33 Squadron)

Groundcrew on 41 Squadron prepare Javelin FAW 4 (XA767) 'K' for start-up on the flight line at RAF Wattisham. The airman on the left is removing the cockpit-access ladder which hooked-over the intake for the left-hand engine. (RAF Museum)

45 and 47,000ft) to North American F-100 Super Sabres and McDonnell F-101 Voodoos.

The following month it was the turn of 85 Squadron to visit the Mediterranean, with a two-week detachment to Malta for Exercise *Maltex*. The squadron deployed eight Javelins via Orange on 14 May, supported by a Blackburn Beverley from Transport Command and a civilian Vickers Viscount chartered from Transair. The first week was spent training with the Malta-based radar unit, but early plans turned out to be somewhat over-optimistic: it transpired that the Malta radars could not control more than two aircraft at a time, or anything above 30,000ft. The exercise ran from 25 to 27 May, with a morning and afternoon phase each day. However, it was soon clear that the Javelins could not rely on GCI to scramble them in time to intercept raids, so instead they employed standing patrols. In this they were reasonably successful.

Foreign travels continued with squadron exchanges – 46 Squadron enjoyed a week-long exchange with the French Air Force squadron EC3/30, based at Tours, which flew the SNCASO (Sud-Aviation) Vautour, while 41 Squadron exchanged with 3 Squadron, another Javelin unit at Geilenkirchen.

Groundcrew prepare to refuel a Javelin FAW 4of 41 Squadron. With full ventral tanks, the FAW 4 could carry just over 1,200 gallons of fuel, while the FAW 5 had a capacity of 1,455 gallons. (RAF Museum)

Ingpen Trophy

During the 1950s there were a number of annual competitions to find the 'most proficient squadron' in each role. Fighter Command's day fighter units competed for the Dacre Trophy, while the night/all-weather fighter squadrons competed for the Ingpen Trophy. Both competitions involved ciné, air-to-air gunnery and Operational Turn Rounds (OTRs) all of which were scored. The first Javelin squadron to compete in the Ingpen Trophy was 46 Squadron, who came third in 1957. The following year the Javelins of 46 and 151 Squadrons both competed, finishing second and third respectively, behind the winning Meteor team from 85 Squadron. In June 1959 the competition was between the three Javelin teams from 25, 46 and 151 Squadrons. This time the competition was held on 'neutral territory' at Horsham St Faith. By the end of the first day's ciné phase, 25 Squadron was leading the field by 47 points. There was drama the next day for the 151 Squadron team during the air-to-air gunnery phase, when they were plagued with radar-ranging problems and finished last. However, some excellent shooting by 46 Squadron helped them to overtake 25 Squadron in the overall scoring, and put them in first place to win the trophy.

Counting the holes in the air-to-air flags during the Ingpen Trophy held at RAF Horsham St Faith in June 1959. Air Chief Marshal Sir Thomas Pike, GCB, CBE, DFC*, (AOC-in-C, Fighter Command) is in the group on the left, while in the group of 46 Squadron personnel on the right, Wg Cdr F.B. Sowrey has his back to the camera. (F.B. Sowrey)

The victorious 46 Squadron team pose, in crews, with the Ingpen Trophy. The pilots, standing left to right: Flt Lt T.F. Carter, Wg Cdr F. B. Sowrey, Flt Lt G. Bradshaw, and Flt Lt J. Jarvis. Front row (nav/rads): Flt Sgt G.M. Warden, Flt Lt R. Dawes, Flt Sgt P. Winslade, and Sgt T. Ogden. (F.B. Sowrey)

Exercise *Mandate*

Fighter Command's annual exercise for 1959 was codenamed *Mandate*. It followed from Exercise *Buckboard*, a one-day exercise which was held in early April, which was designed to practise a new tactic developed by the CFE known as the 'loiter technique.' Traditionally, under 'normal' operations, Javelin crews would expect 'close control' from the GCI controller to vector them towards a specific target; however in conditions of mass raids, and particularly if there was any communications or radar jamming, this was simply impractical. The new tactic was designed to cope by launching fighters to predetermined 'gates' where they would loiter in a racetrack pattern. The GCI controller would then broadcast the positions of incoming enemy raids and the fighter crews would then use that information to carry-out their own interceptions. The technique was practised again just before Exercise *Mandate* in a number of individual group-run exercises.

Inherited from 89 Squadron, Javelin FAW 6 XH694/A wears the colours of 85 Squadron: a white octagon superimposed on a red and black chequerboard. The squadron moved to West Malling in late summer 1959.. (RAF Museum)

Exercise *Mandate* started at 01:00hrs on 23 July and each unit started to generate armed aircraft. Nearly all of Fighter Command's ten Javelin squadrons were available for the exercise: 23 Squadron [FAW 7 at Leuchars], 25 Squadron [FAW 7 at Waterbeach], 29 Squadron [FAW 6 at Leuchars], 33 Squadron [FAW 7 at RAF Middleton St George], 41 Squadron [FAW 5 at RAF Wattisham], 46 Squadron [FAW 2 at Waterbeach], 72 Squadron [FAW 7 at RAF Leconfield], 85 Squadron [FAW 6 at Stradishall] and 151 Squadron [FAW 5 at Leuchars]. The only absentee was 64 Squadron, whose two-month detachment to Cyprus had started in June. However, their place in the order of battle was taken by 219 (Reserve) Squadron, which was formed at RAF West Raynham for the duration of the exercise with the Javelin crews from the CFE using their FAW 5 aircraft. In fact the newest front line Javelin unit, 72 Squadron, was only able to participate in the exercise during daylight hours because of its lack of experience on type. Unlike the previous years' exercises, *Mandate* was not 'phased' so, in the expectation of continuous activity, aircrew and groundcrew lived in their squadron buildings throughout the exercise. This also meant, as the 151 Squadron diarist pointed out, that crews spent many hours at cockpit readiness, often with little flying to show for their pains.

The first scrambles came at 07:00hrs on 23 July. During *Mandate*, Javelins were flown with full ventral tanks, enabling most interceptions to take place 160 to 170 miles off the coast. On the first day crews generally enjoyed 'close control' from

A formation of Javelin FAW 7s from 64 Squadron based at RAF Duxford on a photographic-shoot for The Aeroplane magazine on 8 May 1959. The nearest aircraft XH791 'P' is flown by Flt Lt D.G. Headley. (D.G. Headley)

GCI, but jamming was introduced during the course of the day; by the second day there was widespread jamming and GCI had resorted to broadcast control. For 41 Squadron the exercise was, 'disappointing due to the small number of raids that the squadron was employed against.' This observation was confirmed by Fg Off E. Durham, a pilot on 85 Squadron, 'I flew just one sortie on Exercise *Mandate* on 25 July from Stradishall... we intercepted a formation of four CF-100s.' Indeed *Mandate* was probably an indication of the future of large exercises: gone were the days of mass dogfights, to be replaced with more serious affairs which concentrated more on the issues of command and control during and after a nuclear exchange. As Flt Lt A.W.A. Wright of 46 Squadron put it, 'an exercise was an exercise was an exercise.'

On the night of 24/25 July, Leuchars was 'exercise destroyed' and its squadrons were redeployed: 151 Squadron joined 72 Squadron at Leconfield, while 29 Squadron flew to Middleton St George where it joined 33 Squadron. Early the next morning both squadrons at Middleton St George executed a survival scramble of all available aircraft ahead of a simulated nuclear strike nearby. The exercise continued into the afternoon of 25 July with many of the GCI stations artificially out of action and most of the flying stations dealing with the effects of simulated nuclear fallout. There was another mass launch from Middleton St George before the exercise ended at 17:00hrs. The crews of 29 and 33 Squadrons held their de-briefing in the bar that evening.

Javelin FAW 7s of 64 Squadron in echelon formation among the clouds of a summer afternoon. Although Javelins frequently operated as 'singletons' or in pairs, larger formations might result from mass launches during exercises. (D.G. Headley)

Overall the Javelin force acquitted itself well during Exercise *Mandate*: each squadron had roughly forty launches and the overall kill ration was around 1½ kills per sortie. *Flight* magazine subsequently reported: 'new battle tactics, to ensure that the enemy was met and dealt with towards the limit of the long-range radars, had been tried and "some valuable lessons learned." The addition of Javelins to the day-interceptor Hunter 6s had helped considerably towards improvements on last year's exercise.'

While the rest of the Javelin force was involved in *Mandate*, 64 Squadron had been flying from Nicosia. Codenamed Exercise *Quickfire*, the detachment involved air-to-air gunnery and ciné work, as well as exercises with locally-based Canberras, mutual PIs, and naval co-operation. On two days in early August, Javelins of 64 Squadron also flew sorties against Royal Navy (RN) Daring-class destroyers. The squadron also maintained aircraft on QRA and there were four Battle Flight scrambles during the detachment. The aircraft returned to Stradishall on 7 August.

Autumn flying

September brought with it the usual busy flying programme, including the SBAC show at Farnborough. Once more the RAF's Javelins were called on to participate in a flypast – and once again Wg Cdr Sowrey's 46 Squadron was called on to lead the show. This time Sowrey was tasked with leading a formation of Javelins to under fly a formation of slower-flying V-bombers, so that the two formations coincided exactly over the president's tent.

Most Javelin squadrons were co-located with a Hunter day-fighter squadron, so that fighter stations could maintain a 24-hour capability. A station exercise at Duxford on the nights of 8 and 10 September used Hunters from 65 Squadron as targets for the Javelins of 64 Squadron, which, wrote Flt Lt B.E. Saunders, 'was an opportunity for 65 Squadron to gain a more respectful, and at times vivid, impression of the night fighter in action.' Also during the autumn, two squadrons, 41 and 33, tried out tactics to use a Javelin and Hunter working together as a pair. If there was no GCI available, the Javelin could use its radar to locate targets and steer the Hunter towards them before making its own interception.

Unfortunately the busy flying programme over the late summer brought with it another mid-air collision, but this time it was a fatal accident. Two 23 Squadron Javelins (FAW 7, XH775 and XH781) collided just to the east of Norwich during a night PI sortie on 1 September. Fg Off E.H.B. Stark and Fg Off P. Baigent ejected successfully, but Flt Lt C.S.T.C. Brooksbank and Sgt G.A.J. Spriggs were both killed.

Detachments abroad continued during the autumn with a deployment by 29

Aircrew members of 85 Squadron after arriving at RAF West Malling on 5 August 1959: Left to right; Flt Lts John Taylor (nav/rad), Paul Hodgson (pilot), Jack Broughton (nav/rad), Ed Durham (pilot), Wg Cdr George Martin, commanding officer (pilot), Don Walker (pilot), Sqn Ldr Nicholson, (nav/rad ldr), Sqn Ldr Pete Deacon, (pilot) commander of 'A' Flight, and Fg Off Dave Downey (nav/rad).s. (RAF Museum)

Most Javelin squadrons were co-located with Hunter day-fighter squadrons. Here a Javelin FAW 7 from 64 Squadron and two Hunter F 6s from 65 Squadron fly over their base at RAF Duxford. Some Wings also experimented with using mixed Javelin/ Hunter formations, using the Javelin's radar to locate targets for the Hunter. (D.G. Headley)

Squadron to Malta in the last week of October for Exercise *Samba*. Eight aircraft flew in pairs via Orange. As in previous exercises in Malta the squadron soon found that GCI was very limited. After the first day the Javelins gave up with close control and instead set up a series of racetracks fanning out from 50 miles off the coast of Malta. In the three days of the exercise the Javelins were involved in over 50 scrambles and collected an impressive haul of claims against Valiants and Canberras. They returned to UK on 28 October, but after encountering strong crosswinds the aircraft all diverted to Wattisham.

Javelin FAW 8 (XJ125) was used for missile trials and is seen here inverted half-way through a barrel roll, while preparing for the 1959 Farnborough Air Show. (RAF Museum)

FAW 8 & 9

The first Javelin FAW 7s were modified (Mod 568) to carry the de Havilland Firestreak air-to-air missiles during late 1959. The Firestreak had an infra-red homing system and the first 'acquisition rounds' – live seeker heads mounted in an inert (dummy) missile to enable crews to train with the missile acquisition system – arrived on 23 Squadron in November. However, perhaps the most important development during 1959 was the introduction of the FAW 8 and FAW 9 versions of the Javelin. The AI Mk.22-equipped Javelin FAW 8 introduced a number of improvements in flying controls, wings and aircraft systems, but the chief one was the fitting of reheat to the Sapphire engines. The reheat system was something of a 'bolt on extra' rather than being an intrinsic part of the engine design: it used excess high-pressure fuel delivered by the high-pressure fuel pump. Normally this excess fuel was returned to the tanks, but the Sapphire reheat system diverted it instead to a hot streak injector system at the end of the jet pipes. In practice this meant that if reheat was selected below about 20,000ft, instead of taking just the excess fuel, the reheat took most of the fuel delivered by the high-pressure pumps, which resulted in a loss of overall thrust. However, it did give a substantial increase in thrust above 20,000ft, which effectively returned the missile-carrying aircraft to the same high-level performance as the gun only-armed Javelin FAW 7. Delivery of the FAW 8s started to 41 Squadron in November, and Wg Cdr D.W.H.

The 'business end' of a Javelin FAW 8/9 – the reheat nozzles mounted on the jet pipes. Above 20,000ft the reheat restored the performance of the missile-armed Javelin FAW 8 to that of the gun-armed Javelin FAW 7 – but at a cost in fuel consumption.

This side view of the reheat nozzles [afterburners] on a 41 Squadron Javelin FAW 8 gives some idea of the extra weight of the reheat system – estimated by the 25 Squadron diarist as 'around a ton'. However, the Javelin was the first front-line aeroplane in RAF service to be so equipped. (41 Squadron)

Smith, AFC reported that 'the Mk 8 has proved pleasant to fly, with no handling problems. Its rate of climb and performance at altitude are most refreshing after the Javelin Mks 4 and 5.'

The groundcrew, too, were quite pleased with the aircraft. On 85 Squadron, Cpl J.A. Roberts: 'quite enjoyed working on the Javelin, particularly the Mk 8, which I spent longer working with and got to know better… there were some considerable differences between the Mk 6 and Mk 8 with the reheated engine and Avpin starter system. This latter item did cause us the occasional loss of a sortie. The cartridges in the triple breech initiating system would become difficult to remove and the "habit" of just replacing the one that came out easily meant that the pilot often had to make three start selections before the starter fired up. The Avpin starter motor catching fire on one occasion was also the cause of the only rapid evacuation I can remember.'

November also saw the start of a major conversion project to modify the Javelin FAW 7s in service up to the same standard as the FAW 8. The FAW 7s were sent back to Gloster Aircraft where they were stripped and rebuilt as FAW 9s – effectively a Javelin FAW 8 equipped with an AI Mk.17.

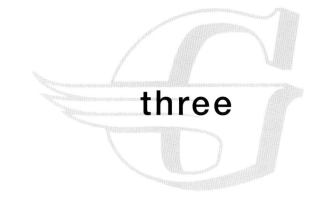

three

THE GOLDEN AGE, ONE
1960

Fighter Command

RAF Fighter Command entered the 1960s with an all-weather fighter force comprising ten squadrons of Javelins. Most of these units were either equipped with the latest marks of missile-armed Javelins or were about to convert to them. At Wattisham, 41 Squadron was equipped with the Javelin FAW 8 and 85 Squadron at West Malling would receive their first FAW 8s in February. Meanwhile, 23 Squadron at Coltishall, 25 Squadron at Waterbeach, 33 Squadron at Middleton St George and 64 Squadron at Duxford would all have their Javelin FAW 7s modified as FAW 9s during the year and 29 Squadron at Leuchars would also exchange its FAW 6s for Javelin FAW 9s early in 1961.

However, the future of the remaining three squadrons was not so bright. Part of the fallout of the 1957 Defence Review was the employment of more missile systems at the expense of manned aircraft and the successful introduction of the first Bristol Bloodhound Mk 1 surface-to-air missiles meant that the FAW 2s of 46 Squadron at Waterbeach, also the FAW 5s of both 72 Squadron at Leconfield and 151 Squadron at Leuchars would no longer be required after mid-1961.

For the first year of the decade at least, Fighter Command had a full complement of Javelin squadrons, plus an OCU, and an air-defence system that had matured with the increasing capabilities of the fighters. The standard night-fighter tactics were now based on a series of lanes, which radiated out from the UK coast, overlaid by the lattice of GEE lines. Each lane had a 'gate' and after launching, the night fighter would fly to a predetermined gate and loiter there. Broadcast control from GCI would then give the positions of inbound raids relative to a

Two Javelin FAW 7s of 23 Squadron armed with the de Havilland Firestreak. The squadron converted to the type in the summer of 1959 and received its first infra-red acquisition rounds in November. The Javelin was the RAF's first operational missile-armed fighter. (G.R. Pitchfork)

Exercise Fabulous/Halyard: *25 Squadron Javelins at cockpit readiness on the Operational Readiness Platform (ORP) on a cold winter's evening. The exercise was not popular with air or groundcrews as it involved enduring long hours of cold and boredom, particularly at night in winter.*

datum and using this information the nav/rad could plot the progress of any targets approaching the lane. At the appropriate time, the fighter would set off along its lane to intercept the inbound aircraft, aiming to do so ideally 150 miles or so off the coast. This system was much easier to operate, particularly in conditions of jamming, than the previous system of close control. Another variation was the use of 'wildcat' aircraft, usually crewed by an experienced nav/rad: in the event of there being no GCI available, the wildcats would orbit at the far end of the lanes and broadcast the positions of inbound contacts. The other aircraft would then use this information to arrange their own interceptions within their lanes.

The system was regularly practised with frequent exercises. These included the routine monthly exercises such as *Bomex*, *Ciano* and *Kingpin* as well as larger Group or NATO exercises or Fighter Command's annual exercise, which was held every summer. Most of these exercises included a substantial amount of radio and radar jamming, so Javelin crews became well used to operating in a busy electronic warfare environment. Apart from the routine training from their home base, each Javelin squadron could also expect detachments to Germany, Malta or Cyprus during the course of a year.

The commitment to QRA continued, too, under various codenames: over the years *Halyard* became *Flinders* then *Flodden*. However, none of the name changes made the duty any less tedious, especially in winter. In January 1960, the aircraft

A dismal looking 25 Squadron crew sit at cockpit readiness. On cold winter nights crews would try to keep warm by using hot water bottles and wrapping themselves in blankets. Each crew would spend two hours in the cockpit before returning to the warmth of the crew room to defrost and wait for their next stint.

An interesting view of the 'nib fairing' of a 151 Squadron Javelin FAW 5, which has been removed for cleaning. The Sapphire Mk. 103/104 engine used on the FAW 5 was rated at 8,150lb static thrust; a shaft from each engine drove a common auxiliary unit which provided hydraulic and electrical power. (RAF Museum)

of 85 Squadron needed to be sprayed with de-icing fluid as they sat at readiness. A solution to the problem had been found by the time 41 Squadron took over the duty later in the month. They mounted readiness from inside a disused hangar, which proved useful after a heavy snowfall made movement on the airfield difficult. Towards the end of the year 29 Squadron mounted Exercise *Halyard* from Leconfield and Flt Lt J. MacLeod noted in the squadron diary that, 'the main discomfort was the extreme cold in the cockpits and a combination of blankets and hot water bottles was used to try to keep warm.' The 151 Squadron diarist also noted that '*Halyard* remains the most unpopular duty of all.'

228 OCU

With the work of the JMTU completed in early 1959, all conversion of crews to the Javelin was done at Leeming by 228 OCU. By 1960, the OCU was equipped not only with Javelin FAW 5s, but also dual-control Javelin T3s for pilot conversion to type and AI Mk.17-equipped Canberra T17s for nav/rad training. The four-month course started with ground school, followed by a basic phase, which introduced

Javelin FAW 5 (XA667) of 228 OCU carries the horse's head badge of 137 Squadron. In 1960, during Exercise Yeoman, *the instructors were mobilized as 137 Squadron to operate as a front-line unit, as they would do in war.* (G.R. Pitchfork)

pilots to handling the Javelin and qualified them with an Instrument Rating (IR). Since all pilots posted to the Javelin at that stage had already completed at least one fighter tour, and since the Javelin was relatively straightforward to fly, this part of the course presented little difficulty. However, the same could not be said for the nav/rads. For although many potential nav/rads were experienced navigators, there were a good proportion of first-tourists who had come straight from the flying training system; furthermore, a proven ability to navigate did not always translate into an ability to use the air-intercept radar. While the pilots learnt to handle the Javelin, the nav/rads learnt the intricacies of the AI Mk.17 in the Canberra T17. 'On arrival at Leeming with four other navigator trainees I was somewhat dismayed to hear of the high failure rate of navigators,' remembered Flt Lt P.G. Masterman. 'This is because of the hand and eye co-ordination and manual dexterity required to operate the joystick which controlled the radar scanner in pitch and azimuth. Constant adjustment was necessary in order to keep an evading target aircraft in the radar sight. Further, the joystick had a knurled ring at its base operated by one's index finger to strobe the target in range. There was also a button on top of the joystick which one pressed to lock onto the target. Operating this was hard enough for a normal person, but it was especially difficult for me as I am left handed. After leaving ground school I progressed to the Canberra flying phase and was soon in difficulty with the AI 17 scanner. I was not encouraged when two of my five navigator colleagues got the "chop" and I feared that I would be the third. However, I struggled on until EUREKA... I suddenly got the hang of it.'

A Javelin fourship from 228 OCU is made up of three Javelin FAW 5s and a Javelin T3 in the 'box' position. The longer nose of the T3 is apparent even in this semi-silhouette view. (R. Lindsay)

'The Canberra T4 had a dreadful smell of rubber, fuel, avionics and sweat as you climbed in which could turn anyone's stomach,' recalled Flt Lt F.M. Pearson. 'My partner student suffered badly and when we got to the point half way through our two-hour training sortie, we had to swap seats from the black hole in the back, side-by-side with the navigator instructor, and the Rumbold [folding seat] beside the pilot, and this meant we met face-to-face on our knees in the tunnel to swap our oxygen tubes. He honked right in front of me many times. He was eventually chopped.'

One important part of the 228 OCU course was instilling a sense of crew co-operation into new Javelin crews. In the 1950s, the RAF's night-fighter force had a *laissez-faire* attitude towards navigators and radar operators. Flt Lt J. Broughton reckoned that in the early days: 'Javelin nav/rad aircrew were mainly treated with apathy by squadron commanders... [and] their ability was assessed from the "word of mouth" and occasion trips with the flight or squadron commanders who were all pilots. The navigators were represented by the nav/rad leader who was appointed on seniority rather than ability.' However this situation had soon changed and by 1960 it was not unusual for a Javelin squadron to be commanded by a navigator; furthermore, the introduction of a complex high-performance aircraft like the Javelin had emphasized the need for close co-operation and complete trust between both crewmembers of a two-seat fighter. The concept was taken seriously enough by students for them to devise their own unorthodox methods of practice. One navigator, Fg Off R.A. Smith, described how 'when we went to the pub in the evening there would often be a challenge for the drive home. Each pilot would sit in his car blindfolded with his navigator in the back seat and an umpire in the front passenger seat. Then each crew would have to drive back to the mess as fast as they could, by means of the navigator giving the blindfolded driver a running commentary of instructions – just as they would in the air.'

During the initial phase of conversion, student pilots and rad/navs were crewed together. These newly-constituted crews completed the course together and were then posted as a crew to their front-line squadron. The advanced phase of the course started with ciné, and then continued with PIs. It was in the PIs that good crew co-operation was vital; as Flt Lt Pearson explained, 'the pilots were masters at instrument flying as the nav/rads poured out instructions and target information… Each command required a precise flight configuration either singly or as a combination. "Starboard gently"… fifteen degrees bank, "Starboard"… thirty degrees bank, "Starboard hard"… forty-five degrees bank, "Starboard hard as you can go"… sixty degrees bank, all as level turns. "Go down/Go up"… two thousand feet rate of descent/climb. "More speed" or "Speed back" meant fifty knots increase or decrease. "Airbrakes" meant we are far too close with too much overtake. The nav/rads barked out these orders in a steady stream and the pilots did their instrument scan to delight any QFI.'

'The advanced section of the Javelin OCU was a typical progression of more and more advanced intercept training,' continued Flt Lt Pearson. 'The instructors listened to the nav/rad's commentary over the radio from the ground (they drove to the radar site) but the most interesting sorties were undoubtedly the mid-course and final staff trailer check rides. This involved two student crews and a staff crew taking off in trail at night. The staff crew joined up in close line astern and trailed the intercepting student crew throughout their intercepts listening to the student navigator's continuous commentary to his pilot. The staff crew then transferred to the other student crew who became the interceptors. You can imagine the excitement if the nav/rad called "port hard" and his pilot went starboard by mistake which tested the staff pilot tucked in under his tail – it happen quite often. The evasion training also led to some exciting situations. The target crew was called to "evade" and went into a pattern of turns, speed changes and height changes. The student crew was required to follow this evasion on radar closing to two hundred yards when the pilot called visual if he could see the silhouette. The target crew then switched on their lights. We were flown with experienced staff pilots for our initial night sorties and alternated as target and interceptor. Student navigators frequently tried to roll in behind the target Javelin too close and had to call for – airbrakes – to

The nightshift of 25 Squadron at work in their hangar at RAF Waterbeach; Keeping the Javelin serviceable was a labour-intensive business for the groundcrew. Until 1962, many of them would have been conscripted national servicemen.

A course photograph at 228 OCU taken in January 1960: Standing far left in the centre row is Plt Off R.E. Johns, the first 'First Tourist' pilot to be posted to the Javelin. After flying Javelins, Hunters and Harriers, Sir Richard Johns rose to become Chief of the Air Staff. (R.E. Johns)

kill the overtake speed. These airbrakes were large and very effective. The target Javelin flew 'lights out' to prevent the student navigator looking out the window to see the target.'

The policy of sending only experienced pilots to the Javelin changed in 1960, when Plt Off R.E. Johns was posted straight from the RAF College, Cranwell to the Javelin OCU as an experiment. The experiment was successful: Johns was posted to 64 Squadron and first-tourist pilots started joining the Javelin force shortly afterwards.

The Frontline

After finishing the OCU course, a newly-converted Javelin crew arrived at their front-line squadron to find yet another conversion to negotiate. Most of the squadrons were flying the Javelin FAW 8 or 9, or were about to convert to those versions; in the case of the FAW 8 the nav/rad would also have to learn how to use the AI Mk.22 radar, having just completed a course using the AI Mk, 17.

The major change for pilots in the new variants was the reheat system, which restored the high-level performance of the missile-armed Javelin to that of the gun-armed Javelin FAW 7. The system was armed by two switches inboard of the

Javelin FAW 9s of 33 Squadron fly in a neat box formation. Although each aircraft is carrying a missile, all are fitted with a full set of under-wing pylons. The stains under the fuselage are caused by efflux from the Avpin engine starting system. (33 Squadron)

A Javelin FAW 7 of 23 Squadron armed with de Havilland Firestreak air-to-air missiles. Although the Firestreak gave the Javelin a longer reach, the extra drag caused a significant reduction in aircraft performance. (G.R. Pitchfork)

throttle box and then selected by pushing the throttles through a 'gate.' Once reheat had been selected the thrust could not be varied – it was an 'all or nothing' system, which had a mixed reception from pilots when it was first introduced into the aircraft. Fg Off J. Andrews of 33 Squadron wrote that, 'the pilots are appreciating the availability of reheat at altitude' but, the 25 Squadron diarist pointed out, 'the extra weight of the reheat equipment in the Mk 8 amounted to about a ton and this, combined with the limitation of its usefulness to altitudes above 20,000ft, at first prompted a preference for the Mk 7 amongst many pilots. Its initial acceleration and rate of climb were certainly more impressive but, at high altitude at which the aircraft was primarily required to operate, the extra punch from the reheats became very valuable, even if its excessive thirst meant that you had to use it sparingly. That same thirst also made a difference to the monthly totals in one's log book, an operational sortie taking about an hour and ten or fifteen minutes.' Wg Cdr S.J. Perkins, AFC, officer commanding 85 Squadron, also agreed that the average sortie length in the FAW 8 had reduced to 1¼ hrs from the 1¾ hrs typically achieved in a Javelin FAW 6, highlighting the concerns of squadron commanders who were trying to meet their flying hour task.

Another new skill to be mastered by Javelin crews was the use of the Firestreak missile. By early 1960, acquisition rounds were being carried routinely, enabling crews to become proficient both in handling the missiles and also in the tactics for firing them. A trial completed in 1959 by the CFE showed the Firestreak to be effective against targets at 0.85M at 50,000ft, which was considered to be 'more than adequate' for destroying [Soviet] Tu-20/Tu-95 (Bear) and Ilyushin Il-28 (Beagle) bombers. The missile seeker heads were cooled by ammonia, which was pressurized by bottles of compressed air, which in turn could provide some seventeen minutes of cooling-down time. From arming the missile, it took about two minutes for the seeker head to cool to its operational temperature. Thus the crew had to be very aware of these timings when carrying out a missile attack. To get into a firing position where the Firestreak could detect a heat source such as a jet pipe, the fighter had to be within in a 20 to 30° cone behind it; two acquisition lights next to the gun sight indicated when the missiles had acquired a target. The missiles could then be fired either singly or in pairs. Theoretically at least, when carrying out an interception a missile-armed fighter had only to close to within 3,000yd behind its quarry in order to engage it. However, the reality was that targets still had to be identified before they were engaged, so during most PIs, particularly at night, fighters were still required close in to visual range with their target.

PIs remained the bread-and-butter of routine Javelin flying. The main emphasis was on head-on intercepts as this was considered to be the most likely geometry when

A 25 Squadron Javelin FAW 9 at readiness: The squadron badge is painted on the tail, flanked by silver and black bars. The diesel-powered generator unit, parked behind the left wing, provided electrical power when the engines were shut down. (C.P. Cowper)

Javelin FAW 9 (XH888) 'K' of 23 Squadron at low-level: This aircraft was later converted to FAW 9R standard so that it could carry under-wing fuel tanks to extend range. Later, XH888 served with 29 Squadron in Cyprus and Zambia. (G.R. Pitchfork)

operating along the lane system. One Javelin navigator described a typical night PI sortie: 'Sitting on telebrief on the ORP at 01:00hrs on a dirty wet night, we are alerted by Trimingham Radar that raids are developing in our sector and we are given updates on our weather diversion which is now down to Yellow weather limits. We get the scramble order, taxi forward which breaks the telebrief, and get clearance from the tower to get airborne. Climb out to our gate is routine and we select reheat as we climb through twenty thousand feet. Listening to the GCI controller as we cruise to our assigned gate (and running some GEE fixes to check our position). We set up the racetrack on zero-eight-zero degrees/two-six-zero degrees and loiter at forty thousand feet. Our controller gives us more raid details and we are sent off to intercept but he wants 'ident' before engaging the target. Some fifty miles outbound with a healthy subsonic Mach number we get a fleeting radar contact at about nineteen miles, slightly low, five degrees to port. Target might be big to get a contact at this range. Estimate target is at thirty-seven thousand feet so its "go down five thousand feet" which should give us a safety margin in the final turn as we attack from two thousand feet below the target and be less visible if we end up turning through him if he evades towards us. Target is converging with the centre line of the radar so it's a crossing target and looks like a one-sixty left to right. "Port hard twenty" puts the target fifteen degrees to starboard and it's now a one-eighty. We could run the intercept as a one-sixty left to right which would need a shorter turn in behind but we might show ourselves (reheat) too early if we turn through him. We need a bit more turn room so "port hard thirty" puts the target out to forty-five degrees starboard drifting out more quickly as the range closes. Levelling at thirty-five thousand feet we are a bit too low so we

An impressive view of Javelin FAW 9 (XH751) 'S' from 33 Squadron, in a vertical climb: In early 1960, the squadron participated in exercises to trial new interception tactics to optimise missile rather than gun attacks. (33 Squadron)

will have to adjust height again. "Starboard… hard thirty" puts us back on the one-eighty and the target is now down to seven miles and well out to starboard. Contact is forty-five degrees starboard at four miles and "starboard hard" [45° degrees of bank] gets us into the final turn. The radar scanner is horizon stabilized and slows down its scan rate as the bank angle increases. We have to adjust the scanner angle up and down continuously to keep the target painted… flying the scanner. The nav/rad has a scanner joystick to control this movement   Adjusting the turn rate with "ease" and "harder" orders gets the target to converge with the centre line as we roll in behind with plenty of overtake as the pilot has kept the speed at .92 Mach. If we started the final turn too late we would probably have needed a "starboard hard as you can go" to avoid rolling out too far behind. "Go up" [2,000ft rate of climb] order for a few moments corrects our relative height and it's time to lock on. Radar display changes from plan form to vertical graticule with an illuminated dot indicating the target which is now two o'clock ten degrees. The range meter positioned below the three-inch square radar

A Vickers Valiant framed in the gun-sight of a Javelin. Bombers from the V-force were frequently intercepted during routine exercises such as Bomex, Ciano *and* Kingpin, *as well as the large-scale annual exercises.*

display is now active with lock on and showing one thousand yards moving rather rapidly right to left as the range comes down. A couple of "speed back" calls gets it under control. Target still moving right so we turn after him with rapid commentary and turn/elevation orders to get him twelve o'clock ten degrees matching his starboard turn and closing the range. Target steadies and turns port. Probably saw our reheat as we turned in under him or detected our lock on and feels us getting close. We are turning port with the target, which is not showing any lights. The instrument scan in the front cockpit must be very rapid as well as the throttle and speed brake adjustments. Closing to three hundred yards with the overtake speed down to a trickle and working hard to keep the target in a good "Vizident" position. Pilot calls "Visual" on an RAF Valiant V-bomber disguised as a Russian Badger. Confirm hostile and selecting guns for attack. Master Arm Weapons switch to Arm. Looking up from the radar set for the first time I see the big dark shape against the stars. No engine glow visible on this target. We turn back to zero-eight-zero degrees for another look down range and listen to the sector controller for information on any targets near us. After all that reheat work we need to keep checking the fuel state to get back to the dive circle with enough fuel for the deteriorating weather conditions at base and the weather diversion. No more "trade" for us so we are cleared for recovery and a rapid turn-round to go back on cockpit readiness. Running the GEE plot again as we transit back to the dive circle. We will need a GCA talk down for landing on this wet and windy night with a fair old crosswind. I wonder what it would like to fly RAF Britannias and change crew in Cyprus or Singapore with a cold beer beside the pool?

Dressed in KDs (khaki drill) tropical uniform, personnel from 64 Squadron enjoy the sunshine in Cyprus in late 1959 or early 1960. The squadron deployed to Cyprus via RAF Luqa (Malta) on 5 March 1960 and returned to RAF Duxford in April after a busy detachment.

Spring 1960

Spring 1960 signalled the resumption of detachments abroad. On 5 March, Exercise *Leprechaun* saw eleven Javelins from 64 Squadron deploying to Cyprus. They spent the rest of the month flying from Nicosia by day and night, practising low-level PIs. Apart from mutual PIs they also intercepted a diverse bag of types, including two Israeli Air Force Vautours. While they were at Nicosia the squadron also maintained Battle Flight, which was scrambled on a number of occasions to investigate unknown radar contacts. The following month 33 Squadron deployed to Cyprus for Exercise *Fawley*, which involved more low-level work. On 28 April, 25 Squadron also deployed two aircraft to Cyprus for a short visit. The difference in range between the FAW 9 and the FAW 7 was illustrated during their return, when they had to divert to Decimomannu, Sardinia because they started running short of fuel.

Exercise *Yeoman*

Fighter command's annual exercise for 1960, Exercise *Yeoman*, took place from 14 to 22 May. The exercise started slowly, gathering momentum as it progressed. The Javelin squadrons were called to readiness on 14 May and there followed

Wg Cdr D.W.H. Smith, AFC, commanding officer 41 Squadron, leads his crews out from the flight line at RAF Wattisham to launch for Exercise Barbarity, *November 1960. The exercise involved high- and low-level interceptions in an Electronic Counter Measures (ECM) environment.* (41 Squadron)

The French Air Force visited RAF Wattisham in April 1960. Javelin FAW 8 (XH977) 'D' of 41 Squadron flown by Flt Lt Drinkwater and Fg Off Donald lead a Hunter F6 of 111 Squadron, painted in the all black of the 'Black Arrows' aerobatic team, (Wg Cdr Woodcock) and a Dassault Super-Mystère B2 flown by Capt Castidien. Sadly, Castidien was killed in a flying display accident shortly after this was taken. (41 Squadron)

a week-long period of 'simulated mounting international tension.' Amongst the developments in the next few days was Exercise *Purify*, the formation of 137 Squadron from the staff crews and aircraft of 228 OCU. The exercise flying started in earnest on 20 May, by which time most squadrons had been at thirty-minute readiness for eight hours. Indeed, Fg Off J. Andrews of 33 Squadron characterized the exercise as being 'long periods of availability with little flying.' There were two daylight raids and a night raid each day of the exercise. On the first morning 25 Squadron launched all available aircraft in quick succession, noting that this was the first time that a Firestreak squadron had been airborne together; the results were an impressive thirty-two kill claims from twelve aircraft. The only problem for missile-armed crews, particularly at night, was how to identify targets from extreme ranges of 4,000yd and many crews were unable to state what type of aircraft they had attacked. Even so, Wg Cdr J.H Walton, AFC, officer commanding 25 Squadron noted that his unit had achieved, 'more than double the number of kills obtained by the greater majority of other squadrons, including day fighters.' For 85 Squadron the exercise was something of an anti-climax, as fog at West Raynham kept them grounded for the first days of the flying phase.

Unfortunately two Javelins (FAW 6, XA823 and XA835) were lost by 29 Squadron during Exercise *Yeoman*. The aircraft collided at 40,000ft in the early afternoon of 21 May. 'We had scrambled for a "stream" take-off during the

Javelin FAW 9 (XH760) 'B' of 25 Squadron armed with Firestreak missiles on the outboard pylons, shortly after take-off from RAF Waterbeach on a winter's day. During Exercise Coldwind in April 1960, the squadron enjoyed 'some light relief from training' and six crews claimed 'kills' against RB 66 Destroyers, F-100 Super Sabres and SNASCO Vautours.

exercise,' remembers Flt Lt P. Masterman. 'Climbing through thirty thousand over the east coast I saw the fin, rudder and elevator of a Javelin spinning down to earth like a sycamore leaf. The two aircraft ahead of us had collided.' All four aircrew (Flt Lt D.J. Wyborn, Flt Lt D.S.J. Clark, Flt Lt J.F. Wilson and Fg Off E. Wood) ejected safely. The nose of Wyborn's aircraft had been torn off by the tail plane of Wilson's Javelin: Wyborn managed to retain some control and attempted

A spectacular cloud of cordite smoke almost engulfs Javelin FAW 6 (XA817) 'E' of 29 Squadron as the starter cartridges fire to spin the Sapphire engines into life at RAF Leuchars in April 1960. (P. Masterman)

A very sorry looking Javelin FAW 9 (XH776) 'P' of 25 Squadron after the nose leg collapsed. (C.P. Cowper)

to steer the aircraft over the sea before he and Clark had to eject at 14,000ft. The whole episode was also witnessed by Flt Lt D. Freeston of 33 Squadron, who followed Wilson and Wood down as they descended by parachute; he was then able to alert a nearby Avro Shackleton from 42 Squadron, which was on patrol some 30 miles away. The crews were eventually rescued by Westland Whirlwind helicopters of 228 Squadron after spending 2½ hours in the water.

Exercise *Yeoman* finished in the early hours of 23 May. On the whole, the exercise was a success for the Javelin force, but it brought home the need for missiles and reheat: pilots of Javelin FAW 2s in 46 Squadron reported some occasions when they were unable to close with high-speed targets because of lack of overtaking performance.

Air-to-Air Refuelling

By the end of May 1960 23 Squadron had eight Javelin FAW 9s, of which three had been fitted with Air-to-Air Refuelling (AAR) probes. The following month (by which time there were fourteen FAW 9s on strength) the squadron's crews started working with Valiant tankers of 214 Squadron, which were based at RAF Marham. They started with 'dry' hook-ups (where no fuel was transferred) progressing to 'wet' contacts later in the month. By the end of July the bulk

Javelin FAW 9 (XH888) 'K' of 23 Squadron, air-to-air refuelling (AAR) from a Vickers Valiant tanker of 214 Squadron; the close proximity of the Javelin tail plane to the downwash from the wing of the Valiant is evident. The squadron began its AAR training in the summer of 1960. (M.H. Miller)

of the conversion of selected crews was complete. Flt Lt D.G. Headley (a 64 Squadron pilot) described the Javelin AAR probe as 'like a dirty great telegraph pole protruding some eighteen feet forward of the right-hand side of the canopy', but as Sqn Ldr M.H. Miller pointed out, 'the beauty of it was that it came right down by your head and stuck out in front of you so you could see what you were doing with it.' Although this length ensured that the probe was unaffected by the aircraft's 'bow wave' it did make it very sensitive to control inputs: the 18-ft lever arm meant a small correction in pitch generated quite a large movement at the end of the probe. Flt Lt Headley found that, 'the Javelin was quite touchy in pitch so you found yourself over-controlling until eventually you learnt to relax.' The target for the probe was a 3-ft diameter drogue, or 'basket,' on the end of a 90-ft hose, which the tanker trailed from the Hose Drum Unit (HDU) in the bomb bay. The technique was to stabilize the probe just behind the basket and then fly up the line of the hose with exactly the right amount of overtake until contact was made. 'You had to hit the drogue with three to four knots overtake,' explained Sqn Ldr Miller. 'More than four knots and you would send a ripple up the hose which would go all the way up to the HDU and then bounce back and rip off your probe; less than three knots and it would not open the claws to grab the nozzle... the real trick was [not to] concentrate on the drogue because it was bouncing around... look at the aircraft and get used to the attitude and your relationship to that aircraft.' Once the probe and drogue had contacted, the

AAR: the pilot's view from a Javelin while approaching a Valiant tanker. The refuelling drogue snakes out from the Hose Drum Unit (HDU) mounted in the tanker's bomb bay while the probe is visible through the combining glass of the gun sight in the Javelin. The correct technique was to formate on the tanker aircraft not the drogue. (M.H. Miller)

A Javelin of 23 Squadron refuelling from a Valiant: The white bands on the hose measure10ft intervals: the recipient aircraft had to push the 90ft hose around halfway back into the HDU in order for fuel to flow. (M.H. Miller)

Javelin had to push the hose halfway back into the HDU before fuel would flow. Although it seemed tricky at first, once pilots got the hang of it AAR became a relatively straightforward exercise.

The ability to deploy the Javelin over long distances using AAR endowed the RAF with powerful flexibility to project its air-defence capability at long range. One theatre where this would be particularly useful was the reinforcement of the Far East Air Force (FEAF) in the event of a crisis. A contingency plan for this eventuality had been drawn up in early 1960: nicknamed Operation Sickle, it detailed the deployment of two squadrons of Javelins to Singapore. However, a large-scale AAR deployment on this scale had never been attempted before and a proving flight was required to see if it was practically possible. The task of carrying out this trial deployment, nicknamed Exercise *Dyke*, was given to 23 Squadron and was scheduled for October 1960.

The work-up for *Dyke* took up July, August and September. It included three to four- hour trips round the UK accompanied by a tanker. Sqn Ldr Miller found that, 'the first problem was no pee-bags.' As this – and other – teething snags were sorted out, sortie lengths increased to six hours. A major step forward was the deployment of two Javelins to Cyprus by AAR trail in August, the first time in the RAF that AAR had been used to support the movement of tactical aircraft.

Crewing into 23 Squadron Javelin FAW 9 (XH894) 'R', armed with live Firestreak missiles, during the Missile Practice Camp (MPC) in June 1960. The missiles were fired at Australian-designed Jindivik target drones flying over the RAF Aberporth range on Cardigan Bay, Wales.

A close up of the red eagle badge of 23 Squadron, as painted on one of the squadron's Javelin FAW 9s. The reheat nozzles are also visible.

The shorter nose of the AI Mk. 22-equipped Javelin FAW 8 (XH966) is apparent in this view; the aircraft was used by A&AEE at Boscombe Down for development work before it was issued to 41 Squadron. (Newark Air Museum)

Firestreak Missile

While 23 Squadron had been busy with its pioneering AAR work, it had also, along with 25 Squadron, been involved in the first live firings by front-line squadrons of the Firestreak missile. The first firing was by a 23 Squadron crew on 2 June, while the second was by a 25 Squadron crew, Sqn Ldrs J.H. Chick and J. McIlwrath, on 30 June. The latter missile was seen to fly up the jet pipe of the Meteor T7 target drone and destroy the aircraft.

After the Missile Practice Camp (MPC), 25 Squadron had deployed, at the end of July, to Cyprus for another iteration of Exercise *Leprechaun*. The twelve aircraft of the squadron spent six weeks at Nicosia practising high- and medium-level PIs, and working with the frigate HMS *Chichester* (F59). The squadron also tried air-

Javelin FAW 8 (XH983) 'S', flown by Flt Lt J.S. Smith and Flt Lt W.P. Sherlock of 41 Squadron, en-route to RAF Brüggen on 15 September 1960. Twelve aircraft were deployed to RAF Brüggen for ten days at short notice to participate in Exercise Flashback. (41 Squadron)

A photograph taken during a squadron exchange to Tours, France in July 1960: a Javelin FAW 4 (XA730) 'N' of 72 Squadron formates on a SNASCO Vautour IINS of Escadron de Chasse Tout Temps 3/30 Lorraine. (72 Squadron)

Javelin FAW 8 (XH974) 'C' of 41 Squadron touches down in Malta, one of eight aircraft which deployed to the island for Exercise Malta Adex on 17 June 1960. (41 Squadron)

to-air gunnery but this had to be curtailed: firstly, because it was causing cracks in the pitot probes and secondly because during the day the upper wing surfaces were becoming too hot to work on. Meanwhile back at Leuchars, 29 Squadron had a more successful air-to-air phase during which Flt Lt A.S. Leitch shot a remarkable 60 percent score. Fighter Command's highest ever squadron monthly average for a Javelin unit, 13.4 percent, was achieved by their sister unit at Leuchars, 151 Squadron, in October.

The annual NATO Exercise *Flashback* took place in September. All of Fighter Command's Javelin units were involved, including 41 Squadron who deployed to Brüggen at very short notice for the exercise. In October, Exercise *Jessie* took place in Cyprus and involved the Javelins of 25 Squadron flying day and night interceptions against targets flying at altitudes from 48,000ft all the way down to 250ft (500ft by night). The 'enemy' included Valiants from 18 Squadron, which used Electronic Counter Measures (ECM) and locally-based Canberras. The Canberras proved to be the most difficult targets because they employed a tactic of approaching at very high-level until they were 60 miles off the coast, then diving down to low-level.

Exercise *Dyke*

After months of preparation by Javelins of 23 Squadron and Valiants of 214 Squadron, Exercise *Dyke* started in late October. Its objective was to deploy four Javelin FAW 9s to Singapore. Two additional Javelins, flown by Flt Lt G. Jones with Flt Lt D.J. Castle and Flt Lt H. Fitzer with Flt Lt D.B. Collins staged to

Flt Lt George Kaye, seen map in hand, preparing to strap into the rear cockpit of Sqn Ldr M.H. Miller's Javelin (XH893) at Coltishall for the first leg of the Exercise Dyke *deployment to Singapore on 26 September 1960.* (M.H. Miller)

*Javelin FAW 9 (XH768)
'E' of 64 Squadron,
air-to-air refuels from
a Vickers Valiant
tanker of 90 Squadron:
The squadron began
its AAR work-up in
December 1960.
(RAF Museum)*

*Flying at low level in 1960, Javelin FAW 9 (XH845) 'N' of 23 Squadron has been fitted
with an AAR probe. The probe caused significant performance restrictions and was
usually removed from the aircraft after an AAR transit.*

Javelin FAW 9 (XH889) 'L' of 23 Squadron air-to-air refuels from a Vickers Valiant tanker in 1960.

PAF Mauripur (Karachi), as spare aircraft, if needed, to ensure that there were four Javelins available for the 'final push' to Singapore. They left Coltishall on 21 September and staged through Orange, Luqa and El Adem to Nicosia, then via Diyabakir (Turkey), Mehrabad (Tehran) and RAF Sharjah (UAE) to Mauripur. The second wave comprising a pair flown by Sqn Ldr M.H. Miller with Flt Lt G. Kaye and Flt Lt L.T. Arthur with Flt Lt J.B. Matthews left five days later and also staged to Mauripur, arriving there on 30 September. Here the aircraft were fitted with the refuelling probes that they would need for the final leg. One important discovery was, according to Flt Lt Tindall that beer crates, 'fitted neatly into the ammunition tanks in the wings of the Javelin, [and when] offloaded after being suitably cooled at thirty thousand feet, it tasted good after landing'.

Wg Cdr G.I. Chapman, AFC with Sqn Ldr J.E. Jeffries, AFC and his number Two, Flt Lt P.L. Tindall and Flt Lt P.F. Harris, left England on 29 September and after rendezvous with their Valiant tankers they flew to Mauripur stopping only at RAF Akrotiri on the way. Accompanied by their Valiants, the two pairs of Javelins led by Wg Cdr Chapman and Sqn Ldr Miller left Mauripur on 3 and 5 October, arriving at RAF Changi on 4 and 7 October respectively having night stopped at RAF Gan (Maldives) en route. One challenge in planning the route had been to ensure that there were diversions available along the route in case of an unserviceable tanker or a broken probe. In this respect, the last leg, across

23 Squadron Javelin FAW 9s, (XH849) 'C', during a high-level transit accompanied by a Vickers Valiant tanker. The most efficient method of AAR was for one tanker to support two Javelins. (M.H. Miller)

2,200 miles of ocean from Gan to Changi, was the most problematic, especially as political difficulties meant that the aircraft had to keep clear of Indonesian airspace. 'The only possible diversion was a small landing strip in the Nicobar Islands,' wrote Sqn Ldr Miller, 'and even to keep this in range, six refuels were required, the mid-point brackets for these being only one hundred miles apart. This in turn meant that the tankers themselves had to be topped up with fuel over this critical stretch and no less than six tankers were required to take off from Gan to see each pair of Javelins through to Changi.' The lead pair of Javelins had made the trip to Singapore in a little less than twenty hours flying time, and made only three landings en route. The four Javelins spent ten days at Singapore, before positioning to RAF Butterworth, ready for the return trip home. During this time the Valiants had continued to Australia where they were supporting the deployment of a Vulcan. The Valiants returned and picked up the Javelins for an AAR trail via Gan to Mauripur. From Mauripur the Javelins staged back to Coltishall on their own.

Over the winter there was a major push by Contractor's Working Parties (CWP) to modify all of Fighter Command's late-mark Javelins with improved navigation aids. The 25 Squadron diarist described how CWPs, 'arrived from Glosters to start modifying all the aircraft with UHF [Ultra High Frequency] radio equipment and providing the structural and wiring alterations for the installation of DME

Sqn Ldr M.H. Miller arrives at Changi, Singapore, after the final leg of Exercise Dyke. *An experienced night-fighter pilot, Mike 'Dusty' Miller commanded the JMTU and later commanded 60 Squadron Javelins and RAF Gütersloh (Lightning F2As); he retired from the RAF with the rank of Air Commodore. (M.H. Miller)*

[Distance Measuring Equipment]. The UHF was very welcome as VHF [Very High Frequency radios] had been giving a lot of trouble both with excessive fading and frequent unserviceability. The DME was for use in support of the radio compass during the squadron's frequent detachments to Cyprus and back. It would be particularly useful on the route flying where, hitherto, the radio compass alone had been a somewhat sparse navigation aid... when the CWP got into its stride the hangar began looking like a breaker's yard.'

Meanwhile, 64 Squadron had fitted probes to its aircraft and had started the process of qualifying its crews in AAR. The first 'dry' sorties were flown on 15 December, with Flt Lt Fitzer from 23 Squadron in a 'chase' aircraft to offer advice and encouragement. The incentive for 64 Squadron to complete their AAR workup was the requirement to provide three crews for another long-range deployment in the summer: Exercise *Pounce* would be an AAR-supported deployment of eight Javelins to Karachi. Like 23 Squadron before them, 64 Squadron was simultaneously working up with the Firestreak missile, having received their first acquisition rounds in December. The two Javelin FAW 8 units, 41 and 85 Squadrons had already been declared operational with the Firestreak earlier in the year.

The 25 Squadron hangar resembling a breaker's yard while Contractor's Working Parties (CWP) carry out a number of modifications to the unit's Javelins during the winter months of 1960/61.

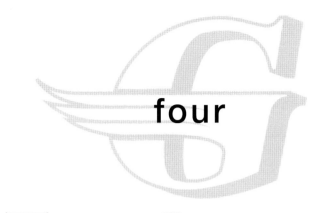

The Golden Age, Two
1961-1962

1961

January 1961 saw 23 Squadron in Cyprus, where it spent most of the month practising PIs and air-to-air gunnery. Back at home, the rest of Fighter Command's Javelin squadrons were also practising PIs, with particular emphasis on missile tactics. The latest recommendation from CFE was to conduct head-on PIs with an 8-mile displacement and large step down height difference in order to deal with ECM deployed by the target aircraft. The height difference could be taken out in the late stages of the interception using a 'snap-up.' The technique was to roll out behind the target and then dive down 5,000ft, accelerating to about .95M until the target was at a 30° elevation above the fighter, then pull upwards. Theoretically at least the radar-laid belly turret of a Soviet bomber could not track a fighter through this manoeuvre. The problem with this technique was that it depended on a number of assumptions. 'They persuaded us that we ought to practise this at night,' recalled Fg Off R.E. Johns. 'You would be sitting there as the target and suddenly this Javelin would go past your wingtip, nose up going like a train, having only missed you by a few feet. You'd be spot on point-eight mach, spot on forty thousand feet, but [the profile] never seemed to work out.' A less exciting method was to let the missile do the work: provided it could lock onto the target, the Firestreak also had a snap-up capability of about 7,000ft between firer and target.

In the spring there were two detachments abroad. Firstly, 85 Squadron deployed to Sylt for APC on 8 April, but they were dogged with bad luck: the deployment had been delayed by poor weather and then when they reached Sylt they discovered that the taxiways and runways were breaking up and becoming unusable because of the extra weight of the Javelin FAW 8. Wg Cdr Perkins decided to cut his losses and

Javelin FAW 9 (XH890) 'M' of 23 Squadron carrying a typical war load of four de Havilland Firestreak missiles. This aircraft was written off in Zambia while serving with 29 Squadron in 1966. After returning to RAF Coltishall on 12 January 1961, following a lengthy detachment to Cyprus, the squadron began preparing for Exercise Pounce. (Tony O'Toole)

The view from a 25 Squadron Javelin being flown over London in June 1961: The tower of the Palace of Westminster is visible ahead of the wing, with Millbank and Lambeth Bridge on the right of the photograph. Note the vortex generators above the wing leading edge.

Javelin FAW 9 XH884 'C' of 25 Squadron seen over London; formal flypasts were a feature of routine tasking, but more typical flying for 25 Squadron in early 1961 was practising 'snap-up' interceptions.

decamped instead to Geilenkirchen. Here the squadron continued its APC and also mounted Battle Flight. The squadron diary boasted, 'we brought up the Russians and scrambled and climbed to height in half the time normally taken by the 2 TAF fighter squadrons.'

Secondly, 64 Squadron started a two-month detachment to Cyprus. The aircraft flew to Cyprus over three days in three sections of four aircraft. The first to leave Duxford, on 4 April, was Red Section, which included the squadron's Javelin T3 and which staged out via Orange, Luqa and Souda Bay (Crete). Two days later, Blue Section departed and met up with three tankers from Marham, under control from Wartling Radar. The Javelins were carrying inert (dummy) missiles for this flight, so their fuel burn was higher than had been experienced on previous AAR trails. After transferring the extra fuel the tankers returned to Marham, leaving the Javelins to press on towards their second tanker bracket over the north coast of Sicily. Here they rendezvoused with another tanker cell, which had taken off from Idris [Libya]. After refuelling for the second time, the Javelins arrived in Nicosia after a five-hour flight. Green Section followed Blue's route the next day and by the evening of 7 April the entire squadron was in position at Nicosia, including aircraft standing readiness for night Battle Flight. The squadron carried out its usual programme of PIs and air-to-air gunnery.

On 4 May, Fg Off Johns and Flt Lt D.G. Holes (FAW 9, XH871) were in the middle of an air-to-air gunnery sortie. As he rolled into his attack, Johns felt that, 'the stick was stuck in the fore-and-aft plane... I had aileron control, but in pitch

I could not move it, it was absolutely solid. We were going up like a train, so I rolled and back we came down, so I started doing this series of huge barrel rolls.' Eventually by experimenting with the throttles, Johns was able to recover to straight and level flight. He was ordered to fly towards Akrotiri Bay and, once there, to point the aircraft out to sea and eject. However, by the time he reached Akrotiri he 'had had lots and lots of time to think about it... there was a little control through the elevator trim and using airbrakes I got the speed below two hundred knots, I got the gear down and I discovered that by fiddling around I could actually achieve a just about steady rate of descent.' The crew decided that rather than eject they would attempt a landing at Akrotiri, which was having its formal AOC-in-C's inspection that day. After a long straight approach, the Javelin hit the runway hard at 165knots and bounced high, but then it settled back onto the runway and the crew was able to taxi off. Meanwhile, the AOC-in-C's parade was thrown into chaos as firemen, medics and other members of the emergency services scattered from the parade ground at the sound of the crash alarm. The fault was due to a loose screw, which had jammed in the elevator control linkage. A few days later the Javelins were grounded for a check of the ejection seats and serious faults were found with both Johns' and Holes' seats.

A similar incident happened to Flt Lt A.L. Button some months later during an AAR sortie off the Scottish coast. As he left the tanker on 11 December,

A pair of 25 Squadron Javelin FAW 9s launch for a training sortie from RAF Waterbeach. During February 1961, the squadron also mounted 'battle fourships' whenever the weather allowed. (C.P. Cowper)

An English Electric Canberra B(I)8 in the gunsight of a 25 Squadron Javelin during Exercise Matador *which took place in May 1961. In three raids on consecutive days the squadron claimed ninety-three 'kills'.*

Flt Lt Button found that his aileron control was severely limited. Then, during the diversion back to Leuchars, the ailerons locked up completely. Managing to control the aircraft in roll by using the rudder, he landed safely from a GCA: once again the incident had been caused by a foreign object, which had jammed in the control runs.

Exercises and Crises

Exercise *Matador*, the annual Fighter Command exercise, which was held between 10 and 15 May 1961, involved all the UK-based Javelin units except 64 and 85 Squadrons, which were still at Nicosia and Geilenkirchen respectively. The exercise was a 'swansong' for three Javelin squadrons. Operating from Stradishall, 46 Squadron claimed thirty-two 'kills' during the exercise, which also saw them diverted en-masse to Horsham St Faith when Stradishall was 'exercise destroyed.' The squadron, which had been the first Javelin squadron in the RAF, disbanded at the end of the month. They were followed by 72 Squadron at Leconfield, who disbanded at the end of July. Operating from Leeming during *Matador*, 151 Squadron found that the

25 Squadron Javelins at two-minute (cockpit) readiness during Exercise Matador; the groundcrew can be seen lying on the ground. In the foreground is a cockpit access ladder. By the early 1960s, large-scale exercises tended to concentrate on the command and control aspects rather than tactical flying – so long hours of boredom became the norm during exercises.

Aircrew enjoy relaxing moment in the 25 Squadron crew room during a quiet phase of Exercise Matador.

During Exercise Matador, *151 Squadron deployed to RAF Leeming, where crews spent long hours at readiness; however they claimed fifty-five 'kills' from forty-five sorties. In the event, Exercise* Matador *was the 'swansong' for 151 Squadron as the unit was disbanded in September 1961.* (RAF Museum)

Javelin FAW 4 (XA752) 'F' on 72 Squadron was written off in a landing accident on 2 March 1961; one of the most short-lived Javelin units, it was disbanded four months later. (72 Squadron)

Exercise Pounce, *June 1961: Javelins of 23 Squadron arrive at Karachi, Pakistan. Eight Javelins were involved, including three crews from 64 Squadron The personnel wearing white hats are the BOAC ground staff.* (M.H. Miller)

Sqn Ldr Dave Keats, commander of 'B' Flight 23 Squadron, (just visible in the centre of the group) enjoys a drink with base personnel on arrival at Karachi. With no cockpit ladder available, the easiest way to get off the aeroplane was over the trailing edge of the wing (M.H. Miller)

Temporary sun-shades are used to keep the cockpit temperatures on the Javelins of 23 Squadron under control at Karachi during Exercise Pounce. *Once the canopies were closed, the temperature inside the cockpits soared due to the hot sun.* (M.H. Miller)

exercise mainly comprised long periods of readiness and little flying; nevertheless the squadron claimed fifty-five 'kills' during the exercise. The squadron disbanded in September, a month which also saw the closure of 228 OCU: it was decided that the planned draw-down of the Javelin squadrons as the English Electric Lightning was phased in, together with the surplus of crews after the disbandment of three squadrons meant that there was no further need for conversions onto the Javelin.

Aircrew of 23 Squadron enjoying well-earned beers on their return from the Exercise Pounce *deployment: Left to right; Sqn Ldr J.K. Palmer, Flt Lt P. Wilson, Wg Cdr A.J. Owen, DFC*, DFM, Flt Lt D.D. Mitchell, Flt Lt D. Riorden, and Flt Lt P. Frewer.*

A formation of three Javelins from 23 Squadron take their turn at refuelling from a Valiant tanker. During Exercise Pounce, *the aircraft deployed in pairs, rather than three-ship formation.*

Javelin FAW 9s of 33 Squadron fly in echelon. The squadron markings have been modified to incorporate the unit's stag's head badge. The squadron deployed to Cyprus for an extended detachment in August and September 1961. (33 Squadron)

Exercise *Pounce*, the joint deployment to Karachi of eight Javelins, by five crews from 23 Squadron and three from 64 Squadron, started on 8 June. Movement of this relatively large number of aircraft required an intricate tanker plan. The Javelins formed four pairs, which used the call signs Red, Blue, Green and Yellow sections. Red and Blue sections 'tanked' to Akrotiri on the first day and on the second day Red section continued to RAF Muharraq (Bahrain) with their tankers, while Yellow and Green sections tanked out to Akrotiri. After a short pause the deployment continued on 12 June when Red section tanked to Mauripur, and Blue and Green sections took their place at Bahrain. The next day it was the turn of Blue section to make the transit to Mauripur while Yellow joined Green section Bahrain; these two sections then made the final push to Mauripur on 14 June. After ten days in Pakistan, the Javelins and Valiants retraced their steps, returning to Coltishall over the next six days. Where *Dyke* had proved the possibility of deploying over the full distance to Singapore, *Pounce* had successfully tested the complex logistics of moving a large number of tactical aircraft at long range. On their return, both squadrons were dispatched to Cyprus almost immediately in response to the crisis in Kuwait. With no tankers available at such short notice, seven aircraft from 23 Squadron and a further five from 64 Squadron staged out to Cyprus. Each aircraft was armed with four live Firestreak missiles. This was the first time that these had been deployed operationally outside the UK, and an important lesson was soon learnt. At home it was the usual practice to fit a protective rubber cover, known as a 'Noddy Cap', over the seeker head of each missile when the aircraft was on the ground. Unfortunately, the Mediterranean summer sun was hot enough to melt the rubber so that it fused onto the glass windows of the seeker head: when the Noddy Caps were removed, so too was the glass on most of the seeker head. Meanwhile, 25 Squadron had been ordered to bring twelve missile-armed aircraft to readiness, a task which was accomplished within twelve hours; however, their services were not called upon further.

The second international crisis of the year unfolded over the summer, as the Soviets threatened to blockade Berlin once more. The border between West and East Berlin was closed in early August and East German builders started to erect the Berlin Wall. Two Javelin Squadrons were dispatched to reinforce RAF Germany: 41 Squadron flew twelve Javelins to Geilenkirchen on 11 August and 85 Squadron moved to RAF Laarbruch at short notice the following month. Both units were used to cover the increased Battle Flight commitment.

Deployments and detachments continued during the latter half of the year, including the ferrying of aircraft to Singapore to re-equip 60 Squadron at RAF Tengah. Each month pairs of Javelins from 23 Squadron carried out AAR trails to Akrotiri for short stays, thus keeping both fighters and tankers in practice for Exercise *Neuralgia*, the reinforcement of Cyprus. Cyprus was also the venue for an extended detachment by 33 Squadron in August and September and for the visit of 25 Squadron in October. The squadron's fifteen Javelins staged out to Akrotiri via Luqa on 18 October, for a week of medium-level and low-level PIs. Sadly, one of the squadron's pilots, Flt Lt J.H. Morris, was killed on 26 October when his Javelin

Flying at low-level in 1962, one of the missile-armed Javelin FAW 9s on the strength of 25 Squadron. At the end of the year the emphasis for air-defence operations changed from high-level to low-level interceptions.

A pair of 25 Squadron Javelin FAW 9s line up on the runway at RAF Gütersloh during the squadron's deployment in summer 1962.

Five Javelin FAW 9s from 25 Squadron in a neat echelon formation. The squadron, which had moved to RAF Leuchars in October the previous year, spent the summer months of 1962 in Germany in the latter days of the Berlin Crisis.

Two Javelin FAW 9s from 25 Squadron throw up plumes of spray as they take off from a soaking-wet runway at RAF Gütersloh for their return to UK.

(FAW 9, XH906) collided with a Canberra (the crew of three were killed); his navigator, Plt Off R.H. Lloyd ejected safely.

Germany

The crisis over Berlin rolled into the New Year and with it a requirement to keep fighters available to intervene, if necessary, in the Berlin Air Corridors. The responsibility for the reinforcement of the Javelin force in RAF Germany fell to 29 Squadron in December and they spent Christmas 1961 at Geilenkirchen. British forces in Germany enjoyed tax-free concessions, leading Flt Lt J. Hyland to record that, 'the festive season proved even more festive due to the low price of essential commodities such as drink and cigarettes.' In late January 1962, the baton was passed to 33 Squadron for a four-month stint. During this deployment six Javelins were kept at readiness at RAF Gütersloh which was much closer to the Berlin Air Corridors. The squadron also used turn-around facilities at the *Luftwaffe* airfield at Celle, which lay almost directly under the German Air Defence Identification Zone (ADIZ). Unfortunately maintaining this high-readiness state dramatically restricted flying by 33 Squadron and, to make matters worse, the squadron lost a Javelin (FAW 9, XH794) on 9 March when, after suffering a hydraulic failure, it ran off the runway at RAF Wildenrath and overturned. The pilot, Sqn Ldr D.S. Burrows, was able to climb out, but the nav/rad, Flt Sgt Christian, although unhurt, was trapped under the wreckage for five hours.

On 3 April 1962, twelve Javelin FAW 8s of 41 Squadron arrived at Gütersloh to take over the commitment from 33 Squadron. Three more aircraft arrived the next day. As well as covering the QRA commitment, 41 Squadron managed a limited

23 Squadron Javelin FAW 9R (XH889) 'M' departs from RAF Coltishall for the non-stop flight to Aden in 1962. Although the FAW 9R could be fitted with four under-wing tanks, a two-tank/two-missile fit became standard.

flying programme, which included the participation by eight aircraft in Exercise *Amled*. Their score was eleven kills claimed against F-86Fs. After their relatively short tenure 41 Squadron handed over to 25 Squadron on 26 May. The tension over Berlin had died down a little in the autumn, so 25 Squadron was not immediately replaced when they finished their duties at Gütersloh in August, but 85 Squadron sent eight aircraft to Celle for Exercise *Quicksand* in the first week of September. In fact a longer-term solution to the 'fighter shortage' in RAF Germany would be provided in the winter by replacing their gun-armed aircraft with the missile-armed Javelin FAW 9s of 25 and 33 Squadrons.

Long-Range Developments

During early 1962, 64 Squadron continued the monthly AAR trails to Cyprus, which 23 Squadron had started the previous year. Sqn Ldr V.J. Morgan also tried AAR from a Fleet Air Arm Sea Vixen on 22 March. Continuing to consolidate their skills, 23 Squadron trailed twelve aircraft out to Cyprus on 6 April for Exercise *Sunup*, their APC. While they were in Cyprus, the squadron also participated in the local air-defence Exercise *Cyprex*, which provided lots

A Blackburn Beverly C1 of 84 Squadron frames Wg Cdr Owen's Javelin FAW 9R as he taxies into the dispersal at RAF Khormaksar on 19 October 1962. The 4,000-mile flight lasted 8$^1/_2$ hours and was supported by Valiant tankers from 90 and 214 Squadrons.

This view of the wing of a Javelin FAW 9R shows how the inboard pylon was 'kinked' outwards so that the fuel tank would not foul against the undercarriage door. The probe light fitted in the inboard gun port is also visible.

A formation of Javelin FAW 9s from 29 Squadron flying at high-level: 'Battle Fours' were often flown when weather and aircraft availability permitted, as the Javelin force truly became an 'All-Weather' fighter. (P. Masterman)

of practice at low-level interception; 23 Squadron also sent two Javelins from Nicosia to RAF Khormaksar (Aden) via El Adem, with assistance of Valiant tankers from 90 and 214 Squadrons. There was a brief suspension of Javelin AAR in mid-1962 as aircraft left the squadrons and were returned to Glosters for modification into the 'long-range' version, the Javelin FAW 9R (R – Range). This entailed changes to the fuel system and wing pylons so that the aircraft could carry a 230-gallon fuel drop tank on each of the under-wing pylons. The modification programme caused some frustration to the squadrons as they were left short of aircraft while theirs were away with the manufacturers: as a stop-gap, the four Javelin FAW 7s which had been used by the Guided Weapons Development Squadron (GWDS) at RAF Valley were loaned to 23 Squadron as temporary replacements in May. Other aircraft were impressed into service too and by August the unit had six FAW 7s on strength; these aircraft were then passed on to 64 Squadron the following month.

On 19 October, Wg Cdr A.J. Owen, OC 23 Squadron, and his navigator Sqn Ldr J.K. Palmer led a section of three (the two other crews were Flt Lts P. Wilson/D. Mitchell and Flt Lts J.C. Bryce/J.C. Chitson) of the 'new' Javelin FAW 9Rs non-stop from Coltishall to Aden for tropical trials of the under-wing tanks; supported by the Valiant tankers of 90 and 214 Squadrons, this 8½ hour flight covering some 4,000 miles was the longest flight attempted to date by Javelins. Back at home, the squadron also tried out long-range high-level PIs in a two-tank and two-missile fit. In another trial on 18/19 December, 23 Squadron flew night-time AAR sorties.

Javelin FAW 9 (XH792) 'A' of 29 Squadron photographed at high-level. The aircraft had previously been on the strength of 64 Squadron and does not yet carry the markings of 29 Squadron. (P. Masterman)

Part of the modification to FAW 9R configuration involved the removal of the inner guns from the wings: instead a light was fitted into the unused starboard inner gun port to illuminate the drogue.

Routines, Checks and Measures

In the mid–1960s, the routine flying for a Javelin squadron remained, as it had always been, PI sorties. Aircraft typically operated as pairs, taking it in turns to act as fighter and target; they might also practise ciné profiles. However, as Fg Off R.E. Johns of 64 Squadron explains: 'once we had done boring PIs and a bit of ciné

Five Javelins of 25 Squadron taxi past the fire section at RAF Middleton St George during a deployment for Exercise Ciano on 5 February 1962. Javelin squadrons were frequently deployed as small detachments to other bases for routine exercises.

weave, we used to do one-versus-one.' Although air-combat training had not been encouraged in the early years of the Javelin, it had since been recognized that a truly all-weather fighter would also need to be able to look after itself in good weather in the air-to-air arena. Flt Lt R.A.R. Carrey reckoned that, 'while not in the same league as the Hunter as a dog-fighting aircraft, a well-handled Javelin could defend itself well enough to survive in combat and make its escape.' The aircraft also flew in larger tactical formations, such as four-ships and 64 Squadron had also devised their own method of using three aircraft to get the most out of PI training: the first Javelin would fly 200 miles down the lane and then turn back towards the coast. The second aircraft would then set off down the lane and intercept the first one, and then continue further along the lane before turning back. Meanwhile the third aircraft would have left its gate in time to intercept the first aircraft and then the second one. The squadron diarist thought that this system 'made a pleasant change from normal PIs and [was] good practice at lane flying.'

Routine exercises such as *Bomex*, *Ciano* continued, joined by other flying tasks such as *Razor's Edge*, *Barbarity* and *Spellbound*, each of which brought a slightly different nuance to air-defence tactics. Other exercises such as *Quicktrain* and *Kingpin* were aircraft generation exercises, designed to ensure that the maximum number of aircraft could be brought to combat readiness in the shortest possible time.

Javelin crews were also rostered for the Javelin Survival and Emergencies (JSE) course, which was held at Leuchars. The week-long course included a refresher of (and live practice at) sea survival and also a number of sorties in the Javelin flight simulator to practice different emergency procedures. A more involved post-graduate training course was the All Weather Fighter Leaders' School (AWFLS)

Javelin FAW 9 (XH767) 'A' of 25 Squadron somewhere over the North Sea: In March 1962, the squadron took part in Exercise Spellbound *which involved intercepts against high-speed Vulcans and Victors flying at high altitude. This aircraft was transferred to 11 Squadron when the Javelins of 25 Squadron were reallocated to Germany in late 1962.*

Crewing into Javelin T3s of the Fighter Command Instrument Rating Squadron (FCIRS), the front cockpit of the T3 was much further ahead of the engine intakes than that of the fighter versions. A Javelin squadron could expect a visit from IRS each year. (C.P. Cowper)

Course, which was run at West Raynham under the auspices of the All Weather Fighter Combat School (AWFCS) which was part of the CFE. 'The idea,' according to Flt Lt J. Broughton, 'was that squadrons would "volunteer" their most proficient aircrew to undergo leadership, combat and weapons training over a twelve-week period and return to their squadron as disciples for the latest leadership and combat techniques and improve standards. The ciné phase lasted nearly a month progressing from medium to high level [40,000ft] followed by the Practice Interception Phase

Many Javelins were used for research and development work. Gp Capt D.P. Hanafin, CBE, DFC, AFC walks in from a sortie in the Institute of Aviation Medicine (IAM) Javelin FAW 6 (XA831) at RAE Farnborough. (FAST Archive)

(PIP) [45,000ft] including some more ciné. More complex interceptions followed including jamming, ECM and window (thanks to the USAF). Further advanced fighter work battle formation and combat tail chases.' The course culminated, in conjunction with the Day Fighter Leaders' School (DFLS) Course in a fighter sweep across the Netherlands and Germany to Gütersloh. After graduating from AWFCS and completing his tour on 85 Squadron, Flt Lt Broughton returned to West Raynham to join the staff of AWFCS, where another staff member was Flt Lt M. E. O. Haggerty. 'Somehow,' recalled Flt Lt Broughton, 'Mike obtained a copy of the tactics manual for the [Convair] F-102 [Delta Dagger]. As far as we were concerned this document was manna. Until then the standard term used by the nav/rad during interceptions was that you turned in behind a target "when it looked right" on the radar. Of course no two navigators could agree when it "looked right" and furthermore it was not knowledge that could be passed on. The F-102 bible took the "guessing" out of the equation. For interception purposes we adapted the geometry and came up with a set of ideal position indicators which when followed took the gamble out of the interception equation. This proved so beneficial that we were able to change the tactics employed in other areas over the months.'

Every fighter squadron would also expect periodic visits from the Fighter Command Instrument Rating Squadron (FCIRS), who would visit to check on the standard of pilots' instrument flying. Later this would be done by the Javelin Standardization Team (JST), which was part of 226 OCU. Another visiting unit was the AWFCS, which periodically flew with front-line squadrons. These visits were mutually beneficial: the AWFCS crews could pass on the latest thoughts on tactics to squadron crews, and at the same time they could refresh their own skills in front-line flying.

Fg Off C.P. Cowper at the controls of Javelin FAW 9 (XH880) 'J' on 25 Squadron at RAF Waterbeach in June 1961. The aircraft carried the letters 'JHW' on the tail, being the initials of the commanding officer, Wg Cdr J.H. Walton. (C.P. Cowper)

Javelin FAW 9 (XH776) 'H' of 25 Squadron; The squadron spent most of summer 1962 in Germany augmenting the fighter force in case of renewed tension over access to the Berlin air corridors. (C.P. Cowper)

The 85 Squadron photograph at RAF West Raynham in 1962, with Javelin FAW 8s. (E. Durham)

Changes

Two major changes affected the Javelin force in the spring of 1962. The first was the departure of the last National Servicemen from the RAF. In his unit's diary, Wg Cdr D.A.P. Saunders-Davies, who commanded 85 Squadron, noted: 'the squadron has lost the last of our National Service technical tradesmen and is sorry to see them go: their hearts were not really in the Service but they did their job well.' In fact it would take some time for the full-time professional technicians to replace the expertise that was lost with the last few National Servicemen.

The second major change was the integration of Fighter Command into the Supreme Commander Allied Europe (SACEUR) air-defence organization. The immediate effect of this development was the relaxation of QRA from one aircraft at two minutes' readiness to two aircraft at ten minutes' readiness. In practical terms this meant that alert could be held from the crew room, rather than being at readiness in the cockpit. The 25 Squadron diarist wrote; 'it relieves us of the exhausting business of sitting in the cockpit for long periods.' Although

Gun sight footage of a Vulcan intercepted at high level. A well-handled Avro Vulcan proved to be a difficult adversary: it was swift (typically flying at 0.9M around 50,000 ft) and it was also a surprisingly manoeuvrable aeroplane.

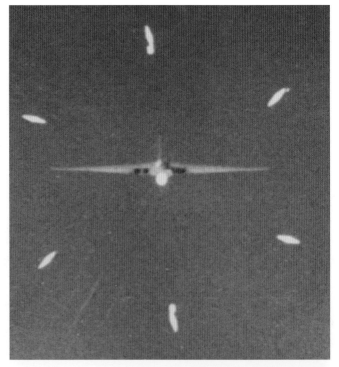

Part of a 29 Squadron detachment to Cyprus: a Javelin FAW 9R (fitted with tanks, missiles and AAR probe) leads a Javelin FAW 9 and a Javelin T3, followed by two Meteor target tugs. (29 Squadron)

Cannon shells ready for loading into Javelins of 25 Squadron during an air-to-air firing phase from RAF Middleton St George; each shell was tipped with coloured paint so that individual pilot's hits were identifiable on the flag.

this new regime was a popular one, there was still some nostalgia for the old ways: Fg Off Johns eloquently expressed the pride of a generation of Javelin crews who had been at the very forefront of the country's defences for the previous five years, in saying; 'you really felt that you were at the sharp end... there you were, a twenty-one or twenty-two year-old lad, fully armed with four Firestreaks and four 30mm cannon, all raring to go. I was very proud of that... I really was.'

Meanwhile, the routine flying also continued. Bomber affiliation had taken on a new dimension with the introduction of the Avro Vulcan B2: apart from its impressive performance (Flt Lt R.E. Lockhart of 64 Squadron intercepted two Vulcans travelling at 0.9M at 48,000ft in December 1961), a well-handled Vulcan proved to be a very manoeuvrable adversary. As Fg Off Johns put it, one intercept in May; 'became very interesting when the Vulcan gave some unusually spirited evasion.'

On 24 May, 29 Squadron deployed twelve Javelin FAW 9s and a T3 to Malta for an extended detachment to the Mediterranean. After taking part in Exercise *Malta Adex* in the first week in June, during which they managed an impressive 92 percent interception rate, they left Luqa and headed for Akrotiri. In Cyprus the squadron practised low-level PIs by night and air-to-air firing by day.

Javelin FAW 9 (XH780) 'A' of 33 Squadron, soon after its arrival at RAF Valley for Missile Practice Camp (MPC) in August 1962. (33 Squadron)

It was also part of an operation to gain intelligence about sixteen Tupolev Tu-16 (Badger) aircraft, which were to be delivered from Eastern Europe to the United Arab Republic (UAR). The first sorties flown on 6 and 7 July were unsuccessful, and merely involved long hours waiting at El Adem, but on 16 July the Tu-16s were intercepted and photographed. The next month 29 Squadron practised more low-level PIs during Exercise *Cyprus Adex*, before returning to Leuchars on 10 August. However, it seemed that 29 Squadron could not stay away from Cyprus and they returned there for a week in October for Exercise *Cyprex III*. This exercise included some interesting close-control intercepts, including two airliners (a Sud Aviation Caravelle by Wg Cdr E.G.P. Jeffery and a Boeing 707 by Flt Lt B.D. Grant) and an Auster AOP by Flt Lt J. Sneddon. Overall the squadron claimed ninety kills from sixty-six sorties.

Meanwhile both 64 and 41 Squadrons had held their APCs from their home bases. Both units had also experienced a new NATO readiness and generation exercise, *Quicktrain*, which would punctuate the calendar in forthcoming years. Exercise *Quicktrain* was a SACEUR-sponsored no-notice exercise for land and air forces, which required all units to be ready in their war footing within a specified (and very short) timescale.

Exchanges

Exchanges with other NATO partner units had been a feature of RAF squadron life since the late 1950s. In 1962, these were formalized into an exercise system known as *Fawn Echo*. Over the summer of that year, all of Fighter Command's Javelin squadrons participated in *Fawn Echo* detachments either as visitors, hosts - or both, since many of these were simultaneous exchanges. In June, 85 Squadron visited 337 Squadron

29 Squadron's MPC crews, December 1962. Left to Right, standing: Flt Lt Davey, Fg Off Lloyd, Flt Lts Douglas-Boyd, Mayner, Parsons, Berks, and Fg Off Smith. Seated: Plt Off Locket, Flt Lts Stowell, Morgan, Wg Cdr Jeffery, Lt Col Eagle (USAF), Flt Lt Robertson, and Fg Off Waddington. (29 Squadron)

RNoAF, a F-86D Sabre unit, at their base at Gardemoen (near Oslo); in August it was the turn of 41 Squadron to call at Gardemoen, and for 25 Squadron to visit 324 Squadron RNLAF Hunter F6s at Leeuwarden and for 33 Squadron to exchange with 349 Squadron Belgian Air Force (a night-fighter unit equipped with the Avro Canada CF-100 Canuck) at Beauvechain. After their return from Cyprus, 29 Squadron enjoyed an exchange with the Royal Danish Air Force (RDAF) at Skrydstrup in November.

The second half of 1962 also brought three MPCs at Valley: 64 Squadron fired five Firestreaks between 2 and 18 July. Flt Lt Headley and Sgt Buckingham achieved a direct hit with theirs, but of the others there were two near misses and two missiles that did not guide. In August, 33 Squadron fired five more missiles and 29 Squadron fired another six in the first week of December.

Exercise *Matador II*

Exercise *Matador II*, was the last Fighter Command annual exercises in which the Javelin force took a substantial part.

Prior to the exercise 25 Squadron had deployed fifteen aircraft to Middleton St George. Meanwhile, the shortage of aircraft due to the long-range modification programme meant that some 23 Squadron crews found that they had been allocated Javelin FAW 5s from CFE at West Raynham. Most squadrons adopted a shift system for the exercise, with personnel working twelve hours on and six off and sleeping in the squadron buildings. *Matador II* started at 16:00hrs

A pair of missile-armed Javelin FAW 9s from 33 Squadron gets airborne. Like 25 Squadron, 33 Squadron spent much of 1962 with six aircraft at RAF Gütersloh due to heightened political tension over the Berlin air corridors.
(33 Squadron)

A fascinating view of the undercarriage retracting just after Javelin FAW 9 (XH844) takes off. The aircraft's underside appears to be surprisingly clean. This aircraft was damaged in a start-up explosion at RAF Waterbeach on 13 April 1962. (C.P. Cowper)

Fg Off C.P. Cowper and Fg Off M.A Harris in front of their 25 Squadron Javelin FAW 9 (XH770) 'K'. Chris Cowper (left)had previously flown the Hawker Hunter in RAF Germany and after leaving the RAF he joined British Airways. (C.P. Cowper)

A tidy six-ship wedge formation of Javelin FAW 9s from 25 Squadron over the sea: During August 1962, the squadron sent four Javelins on an exchange with 324 Squadron RNLAF, a Hunter F 6 unit, based at Leeuwarden, near Groningen, Holland.

on 26 September, with a period of 'military vigilance,' during which QRA was manned by 64 Squadron and the rest of the Javelin force came to sixty-minute readiness. This became thirty minutes the next morning but the first scrambles did not occur until late that evening. From the squadron air and groundcrews' perspective, the exercise involved a lot of waiting around: as Flt Lt R.J. Martin, from 33 Squadron, observed: 'the actual number of trips seems to get less every year, unfortunately for the aircrew… but it is appreciated that the exercise is the sort of thing we could expect in war.'

Once the flying started, the weather closed in on some of the east-coast stations. At Middleton St George, according to Sgt R.G. Evans, a nav/rad on 25 Squadron 'the weather was blowing a gale; the Air Speed Indicator (ASI) flickered above 70kt (minimum reading) whilst we were on standby.' At Stradishall, flying by 85 Squadron was also marred by poor weather, while at RAF Binbrook only two of the five aircraft scrambled by 64 Squadron made it back to base: Sqn Ldr Lomas and Fg Off Johns both diverted to Leconfield and Flt Lt Rixon diverted to Middleton St George. Much of the next morning was spent at cockpit readiness and after a 'blind scramble procedure' by most of the Javelin force, which followed a simulated nuclear strike, some more aircraft of 64 Squadron also diverted to Middleton St George; however, they had found some success in the northern

Javelin FAW 9 (XH881) 'M' of 25 Squadron with inert (dummy) Firestreak missiles carried on the inner pylons and acquisition rounds on the outer pylons. (RAF Museum)

lanes. Meanwhile, Sgt Evans reported that the aircraft from 25 Squadron, 'were scrambled at 00:20hours and [we] claimed three "splashes." Again on standby we were again scrambled at 06:45hours, this time much too early and saw no "trade" at all.' Intercepts by 29 Squadron for the day included a KLM Douglas DC 8 airliner. Most squadrons managed around twenty sorties during the course of the exercise, but at least, as Flt Lt Sheppard of 85 Squadron drily noted; 'all squadron personnel successfully survived both nuclear blast and long working hours.'

Groundcrew on 23 Squadron take advantage of a foggy day to trial (using the crash barrier as a safety net) at RAF Leuchars, December 1962. Javelin FAW 9R (XH848) is fitted with AAR probe and four under-wing tanks; this aircraft was destroyed in an accident in Cyprus in 1966.

five

SUNSET YEARS
1963-1967

The Shape of the Future

In 1961, the assumption had been that Fighter Command's Javelin force would wind down quickly, to be replaced in the order of battle, by mid-1963, with English Electric Lightning interceptors and Bloodhound missiles. It had been assumed, too, that the Javelins of RAF Germany would also be withdrawn soon after 1961. However, neither of these assumptions proved correct: there was slippage in the introduction of the Lightning and then a series of crises over Berlin, the Middle East and the Far East intervened, each adding to the RAF's commitments. Although Fighter Command's complement of Javelin squadrons would reduce to just two by the end of 1963, the needs of the service in Germany, the Middle East and the Far East ensured that the Javelin's operational life was secure into the late 1960s; however, its focus would be with the RAF's overseas commands.

In the autumn of 1962, both 25 and 33 Squadrons learnt that their aircraft were required to re-equip the fighter force in RAF Germany. Rather than simply disbanding the RAFG squadrons and replacing them with the UK-based units, there was a shuffling of squadron number plates and personnel. In November, 33 Squadron formally disbanded at Middleton St George and all of its Javelin FAW 9s, its commanding officer Wg Cdr C.R. Gordon, MVO, and most of its aircrew were dispatched to Geilenkirchen to become 5 Squadron; however, most of the groundcrew on 33 Squadron remained in the UK. The following month 25 Squadron also disbanded at Leuchars and all of its aircraft, plus eleven crews, became the nucleus of a new 11 Squadron at Laarbruch.

On 6 November, 85 Squadron participated in a Group exercise that gave another good indication of the future of the air-defence fighter in the mid-1960s: the targets were Valiants flying at low-level. With Soviet missile technology effectively now closing

The end of the line for 25 Squadron: The squadron was disbanded in December 1962 and its aircraft and most of its crews moved to RAF Laarbruch to form a new 11 Squadron.

Javelin FAW 9 (XH716) 'W' of 25 Squadron diving towards the clouds: The aircraft carries a revised squadron tail marking comprising a wide silver band edged in black. (C.P. Cowper)

the high-level airspace which had previously been the sanctuary of the V-bomber, the bombers had now to try to fly under the missile engagement envelopes. Javelin crews found that their lack of experience in operating in this environment was telling. Wg Cdr Saunders-Davies wrote; 'the exercise was enjoyable and proved conclusively that the way to attack this country is at two hundred and fifty feet in conditions of low stratus and poor visibility. Scarcely any of the Valiants were seen let alone attacked and our three splashes [kill claims] were achieved more by good fortune than good management.'

There was another low-level encounter on the night of 31 November, when a 64 Squadron crew (Flt Lt I.W. Rixon and Flt Lt G.A. Pearce) were scrambled from QRA to intercept an unidentified radar plot. The target turned out to be a Vickers Varsity, which was flying at 1,500ft and just 150kt, which provided quite a challenge to the Javelin crew.

Overseas Deployments

The winter of 1962/63 was one of the coldest on record. In a welcome break from the freezing weather, 23 Squadron once again led by Wg Cdr Owen and Sqn Ldr Palmer, set off for another major long-range deployment. Exercise *Canterlup*, which pulled

Wg Cdr A.J. Owen, DFC*, DFM, commanding officer of 23 Squadron, briefing his crews in preparation for Exercise Canterlup *in January 1963. Alan 'Red' Owen (1922-2010) was one of the RAF's most successful night-fighter pilots during the Second World War with fifteen confirmed kills.*

Fitted with four under-wing tanks and an AAR probe, Javelin FAW 9R (XH889) 'L' of 23 Squadron takes-off from a snow-covered RAF Coltishall in January 1963, bound for warmer climes in the Far East.

Flt Lt Chris Bryce loading his personal holdall into an empty compartment ahead of the nose-wheel bay on his Javelin in preparation for Exercise Canterlup.

Groundcrew checking the pylons before fitting the under-wing tanks on Javelin FAW 9R (XH712) 'V' at RAF Tengah. Before a tank could be fitted, a time consuming leak check had to be carried out. This aircraft was later passed to 29 Squadron.

Sqn Ldr Irving, Senior Engineering Officer (SEngO) on 23 Squadron supervises pylon checks in Singapore. The outboard kinks on the pylons of the Javelin FAW 9R are apparent in this photograph.

A Javelin FAW 9 breaks into the circuit at RAF Leuchars. The view is due eastwards, looking out over St Andrews Bay; the hangars and domestic areas are clearly visible. (C.P. Cowper)

An 85 Squadron Javelin FAW 8 gets airborne for the squadron's disbandment parade in February 1963. (E. Durham)

together the experiences and lessons of *Dyke* and *Pounce*, was the deployment of twelve Javelins to Singapore. On 9 and 10 January, after the runways at Coltishall had been cleared of snow, the aircraft departed in four sections of three. Supported by the Valiants of 90 and 214 Squadrons, they routed via Akrotiri, Bahrain, Mauripur and Gan, arriving at Tengah between 13 and 16 January 1963. After a brief stay in Singapore, all crew and aircraft were back at Coltishall by the end of the month.

The next unit to escape the winter was 29 Squadron, though they were to do so on a more permanent basis. In response to the deteriorating situation in Aden, 43 Squadron (Hunter FGA 9) was transferred to Khormaksar, leaving Cyprus without an air-defence squadron. In February 1963, 29 Squadron was sent to take their place in Nicosia. As a result of this move, another shake-up in Fighter Command's dwindling Javelin force occurred in March, with the move of 23 Squadron to Leuchars. Most of 29 Squadron's groundcrew had been left behind at Leuchars and they now became the ground element of 23 Squadron. Meanwhile, 85 Squadron was disbanded in March.

From its peak strength of ten Javelin squadrons at the beginning of 1960, Fighter Command had, by the end of March 1963, just three remaining: they were the two Javelin FAW 9Rs units, 23 Squadron at Leuchars and 64 Squadron at Binbrook, and 41 Squadron, equipped with the Javelin FAW 8s, at Wattisham.

At the start the year 64 Squadron tried flying routine sorties with AAR probes permanently fitted, but found that they were handicapped by the probe speed limit during bomber affiliation sorties. Another experiment was the four-tank fit (including some AAR), but once again there appeared to be little benefit and a more tactically

In this view of 23 Squadron Javelin FAW 9 (XH793) 'A', the three rows of vortex generators on the wing surface are clearly visible. The aircraft was later passed to 64 Squadron. (RAF Museum)

Armourers of 23 Squadron loading a live Firestreak round onto the inner pylon of a Javelin FAW 9 at the squadron's MPC in May 1963.

Flt Lt D.F. Christmas standing by his Firestreak missile prior to a MPC sortie in May 1963; Donald Christmas retired from the RAF in 1977.

23 Squadron MPC, May 1963 – One: Javelin FAW 9 (XH707) 'T' heads for the range at RAF Aberporth with a live Firestreak missile mounted on the port inner pylon.

useful configuration of two tanks and two missiles was adopted as the standard. Both 64 and 41 Squadrons were also busy in March with Exercise *Barrage* (a generation exercise after which crews were scrambled for PIs), Exercise *Tophat* (another generation exercise) and Exercise *Kingpin* (in which the aircraft generated the previous day in *Tophat* were scrambled (in the case of one 64 Squadron crew, intercepting a Boeing KC-97 Stratotanker which was refuelling two F-100 Super Sabres). Additionally, in the first Javelin MPC of the year, 41 Squadron had fired five Firestreak missiles. Four of the firings had successfully destroyed the Jindivik target drones, but one missile lost lock and missed its target. Over the summer the unit would be followed by 23 Squadron (May) and 64 Squadron (August), each of which would fire another five Firestreaks.

23 Squadron MPC, May 1963 – Two: A second or so after launch, the Firestreak accelerates away from the Javelin and homes towards the Jindivik target drone.

Javelins of 29 Squadron over Malta in March 1963: These aircraft are staging through RAF Luqa en-route to RAF Nicosia as part of the squadron's permanent deployment to Cyprus in early 1963.

Cyprus

In early April 1963, 29 Squadron was declared operational from Nicosia and was holding QRA. However, Fighter Command retained its commitment to Exercise *Neuralgia*, the reinforcement of Cyprus, and other Javelin squadrons still visited the island. After their exchange with a Belgian CF-100 unit in April, 64 Squadron deployed to Cyprus the following month. Four formations, each of three Javelins, left Binbrook on 2 May, accompanied by eight Valiants from 90 and 214 Squadrons. The Javelins stayed with the Valiants until they were 100 miles east of Malta, where they were cast off to continue to Akrotiri. After a fortnight of low-level PIs and some air-to-air firing, 64 Squadron was ready to play its part in Exercises *John Peel*, *Shabaz II* and *Cyprex 4*. In these exercises they joined 29 Squadron and the two Javelin units were involved in PIs, ranging from high-level slow-speed targets all the way down to low-level high-speed intruders. In mid-June, 64 Squadron staged back to Binbrook, arriving in time to take over the QRA commitment at Leuchars from 23 Squadron. In order to maintain the requisite two aircraft at ten minutes' readiness, it took six aircrew and five aircraft, plus the servicing crews.

Meanwhile, back in Cyprus, 29 Squadron was delighted that air conditioning was finally fitted to the crew rooms. The squadron also had a brief reprise from its traditional role when it was required to provide targets for a CFE trial into the feasibility of using the Lightning to defend the island against low-level intruders. Flying in a loose gaggle of ten aircraft at a time, the Javelins flew over the sea at 250ft and 450kt, a sortie profile which according the Fg Off B.D. Grant: 'was much

29 Squadron arrives in Cyprus – One: Flt Lt Brian Bullock enjoys a beer as Flt Lt Ian 'Robbie' Robson signs the Form 700 after arrival at RAF Nicosia on 28 February 1963. 'We were the first Jav to land… much to the annoyance of the CO,' recalled Bullock. (29 Squadron)

29 Squadron arrives in Cyprus – Two: Flt Lt Roy Houghton (centre) and Flt Lt Jock Sneddon (right), cans of beer in hand after arriving in Javelin FAW 9 (XH774) 'B'. The pilot on the left is from 43 Squadron's welcoming party. (29 Squadron)

Javelin FAW 8 (XH966) 'X' of 41 Squadron fully-armed with four Firestreaks. As the last FAW 8 unit, 41 Squadron concentrated on low-level tactics during the summer of 1963, but was disbanded in December that year. (RAF Museum)

enjoyed by the squadron aircrews, especially the younger pilots.' With its return to the fighter role, the squadron decided to place more emphasis on the day-fighter role, a reflection of the fact that much of their task was carried out in daylight in good weather. The squadron started with a ciné phase, which was followed by an air combat work-up.

Over the summer 23 Squadron carried out a trial into AAR using the two-missile and two-tank fit. The trial, run by Sqn Ldr J. Palmer, comprised forty-four sorties flown by eight Javelin crews supported by Valiants from 214 Squadron. It culminated in a night AAR trail to Cyprus in early August. The trial found that standard AAR techniques worked up to around 34,000ft, but above that level the Javelin needed to use reheat in order to stay in the basket; alternatively a 'toboggan' procedure could be used, where the tanker started a shallow descent during the contact. In the two-tank fit, the Javelin had a range of about 800 miles between refuelling brackets.

41 Squadron

Reflecting the new tactical focus on low-level flying 41 Squadron, the last remaining Javelin FAW 8 squadron, had spent the summer months practising low-level PIs by both day and night. On these sorties the fighters would fly at 2,000ft at 300kts, with the targets (typically V-bombers) flying at 240kt. The squadron also carried out a further MPC, again concentrating on low-level tactics, in October. This time the fighter was at 250ft and the target drone at 500ft. The squadron had also been chosen for a trial of a different servicing regime for the Javelin. An extra twenty-seven airmen were drafted into the unit during the summer to try out a new shift system. Half of the groundcrew worked a 08:00 to 17:00hrs shift and the remaining half was divided equally between a 16:30 to 01:30hrs shift and a 00:30 to 08:00hrs shift. The trial resulted in a marked increase in serviceability, but it brought the number of groundcrew on the squadron up to a total of 171. After flying its last sorties in November, 41 Squadron was disbanded in December 1963. Like 85 Squadron, its number plate was later transferred to a Bloodhound missile unit.

Malta

As in previous years, Fighter Command's Javelin squadrons were called to practise the reinforcement and defence of Malta. In autumn 1963, two exercises, *Triplex West* and *Maltex*, were held and 23 Squadron's Javelins deployed to Malta supported by AAR over 26 and 27 September. By the evening of 27 September, eight of the squadron's Javelins were in Malta and a further seven had been redeployed to El Adem for *Triplex West*. During the next days the Javelins operated under limited war conditions and were controlled by the destroyer HMS *Agincourt* (D86) and aircraft-carrier HMS *Hermes* (R12). By 8 October, all of the squadron's aircraft were in Malta for *Maltex*. As a prelude to the exercise the Javelins intercepted Hunters of 54 Squadron as they staged back to UK from El Adem on 10 October. The exercise itself started a week later and 23 Squadron staged back to Leuchars on 21 October.

Centre-line Closure

After a number of unexplained Javelin losses, the most spectacular of which was the disintegration over the Ganges Delta of one of the aircraft being delivered to the Far East in August 1961, the phenomenon of 'centre-line closure' of Sapphire engines was identified. Writing in December 1962, the Controller Engineering and Equipment (CEE), Air Marshal Sir J.D. Baker-Carr, KBE, CB, AFC, explained that when encountering thick cloud; 'the compressor casing cools much more rapidly than the compressor drum and causes fixed stator shrouds and stator blades to foul the rotating shrouds.' He went on further to say: 'this problem has probably been with us for some considerable time, although the cause was not recognized. It has only assumed epidemic proportions during the last three months and the great majority of incidents have been in FEAF aircraft which have encountered cumulonimbus cloud immediately prior to engine failure.' The long-term solution to the problem was to introduce an abrasive compound known as 'Rockide' into the engine linings, which would simply grind the compressor blades to a shorter length so that they could still rotate within the restrictions of the compressor casing. In the shorter term, non-'Rockide' Javelins were forbidden to fly in cloud from November 1963. The modifications were carried out swiftly and most engines had been modified by January 1964.

Exercise *Shiksha*

On 26 October 1963, 64 Squadron started its deployment to Kalaikunda, near Kharagpur, to the west of Calcutta to participate in Exercise *Shiksha*. Over the next three days twelve aircraft used AAR support to stage to India via Nicosia and Bahrain. At Kalaikunda the Javelins shared a hangar with 14 Squadron Indian Air Force, a Hunter day-fighter squadron. Once the AAR probes had been taken off, the aircraft flew daily in an early wave, between 06:30 and 13:30hrs and a late wave between 17:00 and 20:00hrs. Also at Kalaikunda were a USAF F-100 unit and a Royal Australian Air Force (RAAF) Canberra squadron. The detachment was not without its exciting moments. On 5 November, Flt Lt R.J. Wark and Fg Off J.W. Jackson abandoned take-off after the ASI failed: the aircraft (FAW 9, XH765) was subsequently wrecked when it overran the runway. Then two days later, Capt W.C. Driver, USAF lost control of his Javelin (FAW 9, XH871) and spun during an air-combat sortie. At 21,000ft his nav/rad, Capt E.F. Murray, USAF ejected, but then Driver managed to recover the aircraft at 19,000ft and return to Kalaikunda. Murray suffered a broken ankle on landing. Exercise *Shiksha* itself took place on 9 and 13 November, during which the Javelins carried out numerous PIs against Canberras of the RAAF and Indian Air Force, but crews reported that the GCI control was not particularly good.

Javelin FAW 9R (XH887) 'Q', with a typical operational 'fit' of two under-wing tanks and two missiles during an accompanied AAR trail in late 1963. A Valiant tanker and its two attendant Javelins are visible in the background. (RAF Museum)

Three Javelin FAW 9Rs of 64 Squadron equipped for a long-range deployment with AAR support. On 4 May 1963, four formations (each of three aircraft,) supported by eight Valiant tankers from 90 and 214 Squadrons, deployed to Cyprus. (RAF Museum)

Crises in the Far East and Cyprus

Over the course of 1963 the constitution of the recently independent Cyprus started to unravel. Violence broke out between Greek and Turkish Cypriots in mid-December, and British forces on the island found themselves in the midst of warring factions: Turkish fighter aircraft flew at low-level over Nicosia, while armed gangs from both sides threatened the security of RAF personnel. The crisis came to a head just before Christmas and 29 Squadron was moved overnight at short notice to the more secure base at Akrotiri. Unfortunately, the enhanced security arrangements were not extended to RAF families, who were left to fend for themselves (by contrast, all US civilians were swiftly evacuated to safety).

A planned air-combat programme was cancelled and instead the squadron flew sixty-two operational sorties, mainly standing patrols designed to deter the low-level incursions by Turkish aircraft. After a brief return to Nicosia, the squadron was back at Akrotiri in mid-January 1964 and flying was limited to operational tasks. The standby commitment was for one aircraft at two minutes' readiness during daylight hours and for one aircraft at ten minutes at night; for both day and night another back-up aircraft was maintained at thirty minutes readiness. Battle Flight scrambles to intercept Turkish F-84F Thunderstreaks became regular events over the next three months. One launch, typical of many, was by Flt Lt R.B. Lloyd and Flt Lt F.M. Pearson on 26 February.

Flt Lt Pearson recalled: 'we were vectored onto the targets and then ran the usual navigator-controlled turn in behind the targets. As soon as they spotted us rolling in behind, closing fast, the Turkish flight leader obviously called "tanks" as they all jettisoned their external fuel tanks simultaneously and turned hard onto north to exit the area. Their limited power meant they did not accelerate away noticeably but we were told not to engage as they were turning away out of the area. After escorting them for twenty to thirty miles we were told to return to base.'

The same crew suffered two engine failures on take-off within a few months. The first incident was at Nicosia on 30 January, when the starboard engine exploded during the take-off roll. 'The compressor failure was evident by a complete loss of thrust and very loud bangs as the engines disintegrated,' recalls Pearson. 'We had to get out of the burning aircraft immediately. The navigator's seat is located right between the shroud rings which were supposed to catch "detaching" compressor blades. As far as the navigator is concerned this type of engine disintegration is up close and personal. Flames were erupting from both engines either side of me with jets of flame shooting straight up through the fuselage on both sides of my 'bone dome'. I unstrapped from my ejection seat without time to insert the safety pins and pulled the combined canopy back exposing both cockpits. Normally this canopy is quite a weight to handle but in my adrenalin rush it seemed feather light and I had it rattling against the rear stops in a fraction of a second. I then got out of my seat and straddled the canopy to get above my pilot and proceeded to pull him upwards and out of the cockpit. He was busy completing his engine shutdown routine... He stated afterwards I nearly dislocated his shoulders. I was yelling at him to forget the jet and get out. We jumped out onto the port wing and ran down taking care to leap over the vortex generators like gazelles and reached the ground.' The aircraft (FAW 9, XH723) burnt out and was destroyed. Lloyd and Pearson's second incident, at Akrotiri on 20 May, was almost exactly a carbon copy of the first and that aircraft (FAW 9, XH774), was also destroyed. The squadron nearly lost another Javelin (FAW 9, XH834) on 13 March when it suffered a fire on start-up and it was only the swift actions of Chief Tech S.P.L. Slade with an extinguisher that saved the aircraft.

The political tension had dissipated a little by early April and the last 'live' interception was by Flt Lt J. Sneddon and Flt Lt Bullock, who intercepted a single F-84F some 60 miles northwest of Akrotiri; however the target was already heading back towards Turkey at 18,000ft.

Meanwhile in the Far East, President Sukarno of Indonesia had declared a 'Confrontation' with the newly-formed Federation of Malaysia and apart from threatening to land Indonesian troops in the country he had already started a proxy war in Borneo. From Singapore, the Javelins of 60 Squadron did their best to support operations both over Malaya and Borneo, but they were stretched to do so. Initially, the 64 Squadron detachment at Kalaikunda was able to provide immediate temporary reinforcements and four Javelins and crews (Flt Lts G. Sandman, D.G. Holes, A.L. Button, B.C Whorwood, T.R.Gribble, G.A. Pearce, Flt Sgt A.E. Creeth and Sgt F.H.Kirk) were dispatched to Singapore in November. Then in January 1964, Operation *Merino* provided a more permanent reinforcement: Sqn Ldr J.G. Ince led four crews and aircraft from 23 Squadron to join 60 Squadron for a full tour in the Far East. The following month Operation *Helen* saw two more crews of 23 Squadron (Flt Lt Laycock and Flt Lt

A formation of four Javelin FAW 9s of 23 Squadron in September 1964: By this time the squadron had already been depleted by the reinforcement of Singapore.

Shipman, Fg Off J.B. Abell, Capt H. Allbright, USMC), this time led by Flt Lt Laycock and supported by three Valiants from 214 Squadron, deploying to Singapore to bolster the strength of 60 Squadron.

Fighter Command Finale

By early 1964 only two Javelin squadrons remained in Fighter Command's order of battle, of which 23 Squadron had been depleted to almost half strength by its reinforcement of Singapore. Both squadrons continued their usual routine. This now included a new monthly Exercise *Maenad*, in which the targets were V-bombers flying at 250ft. The Javelin crew flew patrol lines at 500ft and achieved some success in this new environment.

In August, the first of the English Electric Lightnings for 23 Squadron arrived and the squadron disbanded as a Javelin unit the following month. Meanwhile 64 Squadron, which had won the Dacre Trophy as Fighter Command's most proficient squadron earlier in the year, received a warning order for Operation *Colastine*, the reinforcement of the Far East on 7 September. The advance party arrived in Tengah five days later, followed in short order by the eight Javelins of 'A' Flight, which were almost immediately put onto alert.

Over the next five months 'B' Flight remained at Binbrook and the squadron continued to operate as two independent flights. The crews were swapped over in

23 Squadron crews are briefed for a final 'Forth Bridges' flypast. Left to right: Flt Lts Reece Sheppard, 'Tug' Wilson, Capt Bob Johnson (USAF), Sqn Ldr John Palmer, Wg Cdr 'Red' Owen, Flt Lts Dave Hedges, John Chitson, and Sqn Ldr Ian Welch.

A Javelin fourship from 23 Squadron carry out the final flypast over the Forth Road Bridge on 4 September 1964. New English Electric Lightnings, for the squadron, had been delivered to RAF Leuchars in August.

Javelin T3 (XH437) 'X' of 23 Squadron – One: An immaculate looking aircraft outside the 23 Squadron hangar at RAF Leuchars in 1963.

Javelin T3 (XH437) 'X' of 23 Squadron – Two: Less than immaculate after an engine start-up fire at RAF Leuchars on 20 August 1964.

Final touchdown: a Javelin FAW 9 of 23 Squadron on the runway at RAF Leuchars after its final landing on 4 September 1964. The squadron's disbandment marked the end of the Javelin's front-line service in the UK.

December, but it was clear that the spilt squadron was untenable. In February 1965, the Javelin FAW 9Rs of 'B' Flight' were delivered to 29 Squadron and in April 64 Squadron was formally reformed as a complete unit at Tengah.

However, this was not quite the end of the Javelin in the UK: the extension of the Javelin's operational life would only be possible if there were crews to fly the aircraft, so the OCU was reformed at Leuchars in early 1966. This was achieved at almost nil cost by using the Javelin FAW 5s released by the closure of AWFCS and reclaiming two Canberra T17s from the Target Facilities Squadron (TFS).

Cyprus

The situation in Cyprus had largely settled down in mid-1964 and over the next year 29 Squadron busied itself with the usual routine of PIs, air-to-air firing and air combat sorties. With all the recent practice the squadron was able to achieve an impressive average gunnery score of 18 percent. Four of the squadron's Javelins also visited the Greek Air Force at Elefsis for a goodwill tour in June 1964. However, for all its routine nature the squadron's day-to-day flying was not without the occasional drama. While descending through 17,000ft on recovery from a high-level PI sortie on 3 May 1965, the pilot's canopy disintegrated, temporarily incapacitating Flt Lt P. Wilson. When he regained consciousness, Wilson assumed that the navigator's canopy had also shattered and fearing severe damage to the aircraft, he instructed Flt Lt J. Cooke to eject. It was only after Cooke had complied with this instruction that Wilson discovered that he had complete control of the aircraft (FAW 9, XH849) and he recovered safely to Akrotiri. Watching events unfold from the crew room, Flt Lt Pearson saw: 'the nav… was duly fished out [of the sea] by the helicopter and delivered back to the squadron… The meeting between the pilot, who was leaning against the coffee bar, and the bedraggled nav when he staggered in was very special… Such language.'

Zambia 1965-66

The political tension that had been growing in southern Africa through the early 1960s came to a head with the Rhodesian Unilateral Declaration of Independence on 11 November 1965. The UK's response included economic sanctions – and also preparations to move military forces into Zambia, a political gesture ostensibly to deter the Rhodesians from attacking the Kariba Dam. In Cyprus, all flying by 29 Squadron was suspended on 19 November so that long-range tanks could be fitted to their Javelins. Five days later the tanks had been fitted, proving flights between

The commanding officer of 29 Squadron arrives at Ndola, Zambia in December 1965: Left to right: Wg Cdr K. Burge, Sqn Ldr Drysdale, and Sgt Hughes with Javelin FAW 9R (XH848) 'L'. (29 Squadron)

Undercarriage leg fractures caused the loss of two aircraft on 29 Squadron during the Zambia detachment. Groundcrew guard the wreckage of Javelin FAW 9R (XH890) 'M' which left the runway after landing at Ndola on 2 June 1966. (via G. Ellis)

Akrotiri and Luqa had been completed and ten aircraft were ready at Akrotiri, in the long-range configuration. Meanwhile the squadron personnel, who had packed for the tropics, were being held at twelve-hours' readiness to move. Wg Cdr K. Burge, the commanding officer of 29 Squadron, led his squadron airborne on 28 November. Flying in pairs, the ten Javelins made refuelling stops at Diyabakir (Turkey) and Dezful/Vahdati (Iran) before night-stopping at RAF Masirah (Oman) and then continuing on to Khormaksar the next day. Two days later the Javelins took off from Aden, bound for Kenya and by noon on 1 December, all ten aircraft were at Nairobi. After a three-day stay in Nairobi, nine Javelins deployed to Ndola in Zambia's 'Copperbelt' to take up a defensive readiness state. Three Handley-Page Hastings from 70 Squadron, provided transport for the groundcrew and support staff.

At Ndola the Javelin detachment was able to use Zambian Air Force facilities on the airfield for its operational requirements, but the domestic arrangements were pretty basic. The RAF personnel were accommodated at the premises of the Zambia Trade Fair and although beds and blankets were provided, there was no domestic furniture, and nor was there any hot water. Furthermore, the whole place was infested with mosquitoes. However, the main problem facing the squadron was a lack of fuel: the normal route for oil imports to Zambia was through Rhodesia, so the economic sanctions impacted directly on the activities of 29 Squadron, in the country. A major airlift operation by RAF Bristol Britannia transports brought fuel and oil into Zambia via Aden, but even so in the early days of the detachment there was only enough fuel for three Javelin sorties per day. The fuel situation improved as the airlift gathered strength, but throughout the detachment the flying programme was severely hampered by a shortage of fuel.

On 9 December, four aircraft (XH848 [Wg Cdr Burge/Sqn Ldr Drysdale], XH889 [Flt Lt Frewer/Flt Sgt Staples], XH712 [Sqn Ldr Wilson/Flt Lt Hodges] and XH890 [Flt Lts Morgan/Fitzpatrick]) were deployed forward to Lusaka, where a mobile GCI site had been set up. Here the conditions were even more challenging: the domestic accommodation in the Lusaka show ground was decidedly substandard, and the squadron operations centre was set up in tents. Operationally, the runway, only 6,600ft long and some 4,000ft above sea level, was close to the limits for Javelin operations and it was decided that night flying was too risky. Initially, flying from Lusaka was limited to operational scrambles only.

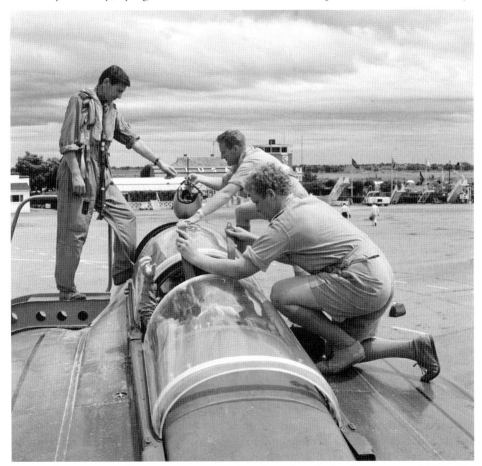

A crew from 29 Squadron strapping into a Javelin at Lusaka in the summer of 1966: The hot conditions and being 4,000ft above sea-level, the short (6,000ft) runway at Lusaka was really on the limit for the Javelin, so initially all flying was limited to operational scrambles. (Crown copyright)

Missile-armed Javelin FAW 9R (XH764) 'C' held at readiness as the sun sets in Lusaka. Although there were a number of operational scrambles, no Rhodesian aircraft were intercepted. (RAF Museum)

Two fully-armed aircraft were kept at readiness, one at ten minutes and one at thirty minutes. Over the next eight months of the detachment, the QRA aircraft were typically scrambled about twice a month, but any tracks from Rhodesia had usually turned south well before they reached Zambian airspace.

It is perhaps hardly surprising that morale suffered thanks to the uncomfortable accommodation and the paucity of flying. In the summer of 1966 a move to the Ndola Adult Education Centre brought a slight improvement in the standard of living, and by then there was enough airlifted fuel to support 120 sorties per month. Rotating personnel between Lusaka and Ndola also alleviated the poor morale to some extent. Additionally, aircraft were routinely exchanged between Zambia and Cyprus so that servicing could be carried out at Akrotiri and this in turn gave opportunities for some personnel to return home, even if only temporarily. In general the Javelins held up well in the arduous conditions, although two aircraft were damaged beyond repair in landing accidents in June – one at Ndola (FAW 9R, XH890) and one at Khormaksar (FAW 9R, XH847) – both of which were caused by fractures of the main landing gear legs. All the Javelins were grounded briefly the following month while the remaining aircraft had their undercarriage checked.

The last operational scramble from Lusaka was made (FAW 9R, XH891) on 11 August by Fg Offs M.B. Langham and R.J.P. MacRae to investigate an unidentified contact coming from the south, but once again the target turned away without violating Zambian airspace. The 29 Squadron detachment to Zambia was eventually withdrawn at the end of August 1966.

Javelin FAW 9R (XH888) 'S' on the take-off roll at Ndola: Flying in Zambia was restricted by the shortage of fuel, but by April 1966 the squadron was achieving some 180 hours per month. (via G. Ellis)

Javelin FAW 9R (XH891) 'R' of 29 Squadron, on final approach to landing at Ndola, Zambia. (RAF Museum)

Two Javelin FAW9Rs of 29 Squadron launch from Lusaka for a routine training sortie. Because of restrictions at Lusaka, crews were generally detached back to Ndola to keep current. (Crown copyright)

Cyprus Swansong

By the beginning of September, 29 Squadron was once more a complete unit at Akrotiri. A visit that month by the Central Flying School to standardize the pilots, confirmed that the long detachment to Zambia had not had a detrimental effect on their flying abilities. The following month eight Javelins deployed to Luqa for Exercise *Malta Adex*, to work against Vulcans from both Bomber Command and Near East Air Force (NEAF). During the exercise the squadron tried out a system whereby ground-crew teams were given responsibility for a particular aircraft. 'They developed a keen sense of being personally involved in the exercise,' reported Flt Lt D.N. Hodges in the squadron diary; 'their keenness and efficiency were reflected in the quick turn-round times and in the consistently high serviceability of the aircraft.'

Groundcrew of 29 Squadron work in the sunshine to turn round a Javelin FAW 9R during Exercise Malta Adex *at Luqa in October 1966. A line of English Electric Lightnings, which would soon replace the Javelins, can be seen in the background.* (29 Squadron)

The squadron participated in a final MPC in February 1967. The aircraft staged via El Adem, Sigonella and Istres, arriving at Valley on 4 February. Unfortunately the weather was not kind and only one of the five missiles allocated was fired: Fg Offs R.S. Barber and G. Wensley carried out a successful high-level snap-up firing. On their return, the squadron started to wind-down its operations. Two aircraft, accompanied by three Victor tankers were dispatched to Singapore, and the rest of the unit's FAW 9Rs were ferried to the MU at RAF Shawbury for disposal. The remaining five Javelin FAW 9s were used in a final exercise with the Royal Navy on 25 April. The Javelins acquitted themselves well against the Buccaneers and Sea Vixens from HMS *Hermes* which attacked at 'wave-top level' and a speed of 500kt. It was a fitting end to the squadron's Javelin days; it reformed the following month at Wattisham with Lightnings. At the same time, responsibility for the air defence of Cyprus was transferred to 56 Squadron equipped with Lightnings.

RAF Germany
1958 – 1966

2 Tactical Air Force (2 TAF)

In the mid-1950s, the RAF maintained a sizeable presence on continental Europe in the shape of 2 TAF. At its peak strength in 1955, 2 TAF comprised of thirty-six front-line squadrons, including fighters, bombers and reconnaissance aircraft. This order of battle included four squadrons of Meteor NF 11 night fighters, which were responsible for the night-time air defence of northern Germany: 96 and 256 Squadrons based at Ahlhorn and 68 and 87 Squadrons based at RAF Wahn (near Köln [Cologne]). However, the RAF presence in Germany bore the brunt of the cuts made to the service in the 1957 Defence White Paper. By 1958, 2 TAF had been reduced by almost half to just 18 squadrons, but all four of the night-fighter squadrons were retained.

87 Squadron

The first squadrons in 2 TAF to re-equip with the Javelin, was 87 Squadron under the command of Wg Cdr L.W.G. Gill. The unit had moved from Wahn to Brüggen (west of Mönchen-Gladbach) in August 1957 as part of the re-organization of 2 TAF. Javelin conversion started on 7 August when the JMTU arrived at Brüggen with their two Vickers Valetta transports, along with the squadron's first two Javelins. The rest of the aircraft, 'second-hand' Javelin FAW 1s from 46 Squadron, started to arrive the following month as 46 Squadron re-equipped with the FAW 2. By the end of September, all the squadron pilots had flown solo in the new aircraft and five crews had completed the initial conversion to type. The squadron still flew Meteors, which, conveniently, were used as targets by crews undergoing the conversion syllabus.

Newly painted in the markings 87 Squadron, Javelin FAW 1 (XA628) 'B' leads a pair of Meteor NF 11s. The squadron operated both types for a short time and used the Meteors to act as targets for Javelin conversion sorties. (R.A.R. Carrey)

87 Squadron inherited 46 Squadron's Javelin FAW 1s: 87 Squadron's markings comprised a red sword outlined in white on the tail and a black and white bar with a green wave, either side of the nose roundel. (R.A.R. Carrey)

The massive increase in operational capability of the Javelin over the Meteor was demonstrated during Exercise *Argus* on 4 October when four Meteors and a Javelin were scrambled and vectored on to a Canberra which was flying above 40,000 ft. The squadron diarist recorded: 'The Meteors were two miles behind and not gaining when the Javelin came over the top and completed the interception.' The squadron was fully established with thirteen Javelins by the end of December. When HRH Prince Phillip visited Brüggen in March 1957, he was greeted with the impressive spectacle of four Javelins flying past at 150ft and 530kt.

Like the UK-based squadrons, fighter units in 2 TAF participated in routine monthly exercises. These included Exercise *Argus*, in which targets were Vulcans, Valiants and 'the more familiar Canberras,' and Exercise *Guest*, where targets included F-100 Super Sabres and B-66 Destroyers from the USAF and F-84F Thunderstreaks from the *Luftwaffe* and French Air Force. Along with the Meteor squadrons, 87 Squadron also maintained Battle Flight standby during the hours of darkness. As in the UK, the crews were unimpressed at the discomfort of sitting for long periods in the aircraft with the canopies open to stop them misting up; this was particularly inconvenient in heavy rain. On 15 April, the Battle Flight was scrambled to intercept an unidentified contact to the south of the airfield. The Javelin successfully intercepted the target and accompanied it as it descended in the Frankfurt area, before handing it over to 4 TAF. The aircraft was later identified as a USAF B-66.

In the spring of 1957, the squadron also hosted visits by other UK-based Javelin units: 46 Squadron visited Brüggen in March and 151 Squadron followed in April. In June, 46 Squadron was at Brüggen again to participate in the NATO Exercise *Fullplay*. The two Javelin squadrons operated as a composite wing for the exercise, during which 87 Squadron flew eighty-five sorties and claimed 108 kills. Unfortunately there was a fatal accident on the last day of the exercise: Flt Lt J.E.

One of twelve Javelins on 141 Squadron deployed to Germany on 17 September 1957 to take part in the NATO Exercise Counterpunch. *Javelin FAW 4 (XA636) is marshalled to its parking spot at RAF Geilenkirchen.*

Breakwell and Fg Off J.J. Jackson suffered a double engine failure and ejected from their Javelin (FAW 1, XA558). Sadly Breakwell's parachute did not open and he was killed.

Another accident a month later underlined the unreliability of the cartridge starting system used on the Sapphire engine. On 22 July, Flt Lt R.A.R. Carrey started the engines of his Javelin (FAW 1, XA559) but as he recalls: 'unknown to everyone, the aircraft had developed a hydraulic leak somewhere in the servicing space in front of the two engines, where all the hydraulic pumps were situated. When the first engine started, and the hydraulics were pressurized a fine mist of hydraulic fluid was sprayed into the area. As luck would have it, the second starter had a hot gas leak, and the vapour exploded with a terrific bang. I was out of the cockpit, and halfway down the ladder when, looking up, I could see the rear hood about twenty feet up above. Luckily, my navigator, Alec Cooper had not started to get out, as the hood crashed down again right across the hood rails, before bouncing off onto the ground. The force of the explosion had sprung the hood off the rails, ripped open a great hole in the fuselage just aft of the rear cockpit, and conveniently extinguished the fire. Rather ludicrously, the two engine intake liners had been blown inside out, and stuck out forwards like a pair of misplaced naval guns. As Alec joined me on the ground it started to pelt with rain.'

The upper fuselage on Javelin FAW 1 (XA559) of 87 Squadron, after the starter exploded at RAF Brüggen on 22 July 1958. The rear canopy can be seen hanging precariously on the left-hand side. (R.A.R. Carrey)

A rare photograph of a 96 Squadron Javelin: Wg Cdr D.W.B. Farrar, DFC, AFC, commanding officer of 96 Squadron greets Javelin FAW 7 (XA750) on its arrival at RAF Geilenkirchen on 12 September 1958. (D. Sanderson)

The squadron deployed to Sylt for APC for most of the month of August. The squadron's average scores for air-to-air gunnery were encouraging, including those of Flt Lt R.H. Bateman and P.R. Woodham, who both achieved an impressive 36 percent. Occasionally aircraft from Sylt might be diverted from APC sorties for air-defence tasks: on 8 August, Flt Lt Woodham and Flt Lt P.J. Walsh were vectored onto an unidentified target and intercepted a Tupolev Tu-104 (reporting name Camel) airliner at 0.8M and 30,000ft. The Tupolev's flight plan had not been passed on to the air-defence network and the Russian Embassy in London formally complained to the Foreign Office about an unprovoked attack on a Russian aircraft. The APC had also included air-to-ground strafing, but this profile was prohibited from September because of the fatigue factor on the aircraft.

96 & 3 Squadrons

In September 1958, 96 Squadron was surprised by the arrival of its first two Javelin FAW 4s (XA750 and XA762) at Geilenkirchen, a month before the aircraft were due to arrive. Like those received by 87 Squadron, the aircraft were 'cast offs' from a Fighter Command squadron, in this case 41 Squadron. The squadron's conversion to the Javelin had already been planned and OCU courses had already been arranged for crews; Wg Cdr D.W.B. Farrar, DFC, AFC, hastily revised the course dates and two crews were immediately dispatched to the OCU. The first operational Javelin flight by a 96 Squadron crew was on 2 October when Wg Cdr Farrar and Flt Lt I.B.

Javelin FAW 4 (XA763), crewed by Flt Lt Drinkwater and Flt Sgt Brown, starts up in a cloud of black smoke. The aircraft is in the colours of 3 Squadron which comprise a red and grey cockatrice on a green bar. (3 Squadron)

Heavers launched (FAW 4, XA750) for an Exercise *Argus* sortie. The crew claimed kills against a Hunter, a Canberra and a USAF Martin RB-57 Canberra.

On 21 January 1959, 96 Squadron was disbanded and re-numbered 3 Squadron, making 96 Squadron the shortest-lived Javelin unit. The new 3 Squadron completed its Javelin conversion in March 1959, taking its place on Battle Flight roster halfway through the month. Another change in January was the re-naming of 2 TAF to become RAF Germany.

A formation of Javelin FAW 4s from 3 Squadron fly in the typical industrial haze which affected many parts of Germany. In 1959, the squadron detached to RAF Wattisham to gain experience of Fighter Command's operating procedures. (3 Squadron)

Accidents

Over the winter of 1958/59 two major incidents interrupted the daily routine of 87 Squadron. On 12 December, Flt Lt K.A. Pye and Flt Lt M.G. Rosenorn-Lanng suffered a double engine flameout at 40,000ft. After jettisoning the ventral tanks, Pye managed to relight one engine at 25,000ft and the other at 18,000ft. The aircraft (FAW 1, XA572) landed at Florennes, where both engines were declared serviceable. However, on the return flight the crew experienced another double flameout; once again they managed to relight the engines and this time they recovered the aircraft safely to RAF Brüggen.

The second accident occurred on 18 February 1959. Flt Lt Carrey in FAW1 (XA569), was carrying out a ciné weave sortie as number Two to Flt Lt Woodham. 'After completing my first attack,' recalled Carrey, 'I pulled up high to slow down, loosening my straps to change the film on the [gun sight] camera, and allowing the aircraft to bunt slowly over at quite low speed so as to end up descending behind my target. Suddenly, there was a bang, and I found my seat rising up the rails. I distinctly remember pausing halfway out of the cockpit, looking down on the nose of the aircraft, and then the main seat ejection sequence started.' Unbeknown to Carrey, the gas seal in the depths of the seat had become disconnected and that had allowed the seat to travel upwards under negative-g until the ejection sequence started. But worse was to come for Carrey, for when he separated from the seat: 'I found myself falling out of the parachute harness as well. As I fell upside down I managed to grab one of the straps and pull myself back to a sitting position. My life was saved by the lower right leg strap which threads through the crotch loop in the harness before clipping into the box. This strap jammed in the crotch loop long enough for me to get my arm through the triangular brace on the strap and clasp my hands together in a "butchers grip". When the leg strap freed itself, I was hanging by one arm for the rest of the descent. I was able to let the dinghy pack down on its static line, which stopped the swinging, and I was able to look around. It was very clear, with a complete layer of what I knew was freezing fog a long way below. I saw the mushroom cloud where my aircraft crashed fairly close below, but had little idea of my exact position. After what seemed a very long time, I entered the fog layer, and it became very dark. I hit the ground hard without even seeing it, stood up and looked around. I did not need to take my parachute off.' Sadly, when Flt Lt A. Cooper, his nav/rad, ejected his seat malfunctioned and he was killed.

Exercise *Top Weight* and Detachments

Both of RAF Germany's Javelin squadrons participated in the annual SACEUR Exercise *Top Weight*, which ran from 9 to 16 April 1959. At Brüggen, 87 Squadron was also joined by 33 Squadron visiting from Middleton St George, while 3 Squadron deployed four aircraft to Gütersloh for the duration of the exercise. In the previous month 87 Squadron had enjoyed an exchange with 445 Squadron Royal Canadian Air Force (RCAF), a CF-100 unit at Marville. The squadron deployed to Sylt for its annual APC on 31 May, remaining there for most of June.

Javelin FAW 7s of 33 Squadron operating from the southern taxiway at Brüggen during Exercise Topweight *in April 1959. The squadron enjoyed good weather and good flying throughout the exercise.* (33 Squadron)

In the same month, 3 Squadron detached to Wattisham to gain some experience of Fighter Command's operating procedures. Sadly, two tragedies affected 3 Squadron in mid-1959. The first occurred on 20 June after an open day at the *Luftwaffe* base at Nörvenich. Flt Lt W.S. Jacques and Fg Off D.A. Ritchie had flown a Javelin (FAW 4, XA750) to the airfield as a static exhibit. Just after take-off for the return leg to Geilenkirchen, Jacques attempted a slow roll at low-level; unfortunately he lost control during the manoeuvre and the aircraft flicked and span in. Both crew members were killed instantly. This accident was

The last take-off: Javelin FAW 4 (XA750) of 3 Squadron leaves RNLAF base at GAF Nörvenich where it had been a static exhibit at the air day on 20 June 1959. The crew are Flt Lt W.S. Jacques and Fg Off D.A. Ritchie. (3 Squadron)

Moments after take-off Jacques attempted to perform a roll at very low-level, but he lost control of the aircraft which stalled and entered a spin. (Crown copyright)

The tailfin is the only recognisable piece of wreckage after the Javelin hit the ground almost vertically, 1½ miles northwest of the airfield. Sadly, both crew-members were killed. (Crown copyright)

one of a number of avoidable flying accidents that occurred in Germany during the early part of 1959. As a result, there was considerable concern at HQ RAF Germany and in July an instruction was issued that all pilots were to be checked out on instrument flying in the Meteor T7. The second unfortunate event for 3 Squadron was the death of the Squadron Warrant Officer, WO J. Brophy, MBE

Cpl Carless and Cpl Sanderson of 3 Squadron looking very self-conscious on the flight line at RAF Sylt during 3 Squadron's APC detachment. (3 Squadron)

The line-up of Javelin FAW 4s (XA630 'F' nearest) of 3 Squadron at RAF Sylt for the squadron's APC in October 1959. Unfortunately poor weather conditions meant that crews could only fire on seven of the eighteen days of the detachment.
(3 Squadron)

who was, in the words of Wg Cdr Farrar: 'a Javelin expert having served on 46 Squadron since the introduction of the Javelin into service.' On 24 July, Brophy who was 48 years-old collapsed and died in the squadron hangar.

Operational control of the Javelins transferred from the Sector Operations Centre (SOC) at Uedem to the SOC at Brockzetel in July. Some teething problems were encountered by 87 Squadron as they practised high-level PIs with the new controllers, but these were soon ironed out. Later in the summer, the Javelin crews practised using broadcast and loiter-techniques similar to those employed by Fighter Command in the UK. During July, six Javelins from 87 Squadron and six from 3 Squadron acted as 'enemy forces' for the Fighter Command Exercise *Matador*, carrying out simulated low-level attacks on the UK. Also there were Battle Flight practice scrambles in the month, and 87 Squadron crews reported that on two occasions they were shadowed by Soviet aircraft flying parallel tracks on their side of the Air Defence Identification Zone (ADIZ).

Fatigue Problems

In late October, ten Javelin FAW 1s of 87 Squadron were grounded because they were nearing the end of their fatigue life. The squadron was left with just two aircraft: a single FAW 1 and a FAW 5. The fatigue life had been calculated assuming 1,800 hours of high-level PIs; however in Germany, where there was more of an emphasis on low-level flying, this life came down to a mere 175 hours. After a couple of lean months, the Javelin FAW 1s were bolstered by Javelin FAW 4s and 5s and in December the squadron was back up to strength with ten aircraft and a Javelin T3. The problems were not entirely restricted to 87 Squadron: 3 Squadron

Flt Lt B. Ibison and Flt Lt P. Marsh in the cockpit of Javelin FAW 5 (XA709) 'H' on 5 Squadron in 1961: On the tail, the squadron's maple leaf emblem is painted in green on a red band. In March 1966, the squadron's battle flight was scrambled twice to investigate contacts in the Air Defence Identification Zone (ADIZ). (5 Squadron)

was also instructed that all PIs should be carried out above 35,000ft in order to preserve fatigue life. The squadron's APC at Sylt in October had been limited by gale force winds and driving rain, which meant that the squadron was only able to fly on seven of the eighteen days.

January 1960 brought freezing conditions, including 5in of snow at Brüggen. The 87 Squadron diarist reported that attempts to clear the runway by taxiing Javelins over it was 'reasonably successful, but not recommended as the brakes tended to overheat.'

The dangers of disorientation during night flying were well illustrated on 18 January by an 87 Squadron crew, Flt Lt R.H. Bateman and Flt Lt P.J. Walsh. Bateman became disorientated in the final stages of an interception at 40,000ft and rolled inverted. The aircraft seemed to be chasing a contrail that was beneath them. Luckily, Walsh was able to talk his pilot back up the right way and the aircraft recovered at 15,000ft, though not before it had gone supersonic over Dusseldorf.

5 & 11 Squadrons

During 1959, the two remaining Meteor squadrons, 68 Squadron at Laarbruch and 256 Squadron at Geilenkirchen had been renumbered as 5 and 11 Squadrons respectively. 11 Squadron received its first Javelin FAW 4s in October, and became operational with the new type in January 1960, the same month that the Javelin FAW 5s of 5 Squadron arrived at Laarbruch. Like 96 Squadron before them, both units dispatched their crews to the OCU at Leeming for the conversion process.

Javelin FAW 4 (XA756) 'C' in the colours of 11 Squadron flying above the clouds: In September 1960, 11 Squadron flew sixty-three sorties and claimed fifty-two 'kills' during Exercise Flashback. *(Crown copyright)*

RAF Germany Routine

The main commitment for Javelin squadrons in RAFG was to maintain battle flight in the hours of darkness. Outside this operational commitment training sorties by day and night would be used for PIs, ciné and air combat. The squadrons used a similar day and night wave system to that adopted by the UK-based Javelin units. Regular monthly exercises included *Amled*, *Bomex*, *Cat and Mouse*, *Co-op* and *Argus*, all of which usually entailed launches from the ORP to carry out interceptions. Exercise *Round Robin* was a cross-servicing exercise in which crews flew to other NATO bases to give groundcrews there practice in turning round unfamiliar aircraft types. Finally, no-notice generation exercises such as *Quicktrain* were called at irregular intervals. Squadrons could expect an exchange with another NATO air force each year as well as the annual APC, which, until the station closed in 1961, was held at Sylt. For 87 Squadron the APC for 1960 was held in May and the exchange was with 151 Squadron at Leuchars; 3 Squadron carried out an exchange with 337 Squadron RNoAF at Gardermoen in May and held their APC in July.

The issue of a Javelin T3 to each squadron enabled pilots to be subjected to their various supervisory checks, such as instrument ratings on their current type (previously this had been carried out in a two-seat Meteor or Vampire). Additionally there was a Javelin simulator initially at Geilenkirchen, which was later moved to Laarbruch. Crews would periodically spend a whole day at the simulator flying one sortie in the morning and another in the afternoon.

Unlike QRA in Fighter Command, Battle Flight scrambles were quite a frequent occurrence in Germany. One such scramble was by an 87 Squadron crew, Flt Lt R.C. Fenning and Flt Lt P.E. Dell, on 11 March 1960, to intercept a contact which was coming in from the Russian Zone. It turned out to be a *Luftwaffe* Lockheed T-33 and it was also intercepted by two USAF F-102s, which then escorted the aircraft to Zweibrucken.

Exercise *Flashback*

The major SACEUR exercise of 1960 was *Flashback*, which ran from 20 to 23 September. All Javelin squadrons in RAF Germany took part. They were joined at Brüggen by the Javelin FAW 8s of 41 Squadron, which operated from the southern taxiway, with tents to accommodate the personnel. Crews of 87 Squadron found the exercise to be disappointing because they were only used for 'standard' close-control interceptions (rather than the broadcast control and loiter procedures which they had practised), but at least they found lots of 'trade'. At Geilenkirchen 3 and 11 Squadrons between them flew 119 sorties, claiming 89 kills, but Flt Lt R.W. Burgess

Javelin FAW 1 (XA628) 'B' of 87 Squadron: In November 1960, the squadron flew a number of 'mixed' sorties with Hunters from 4 Squadron, using the Javelin's radar to locate targets. In January 1961, 87 Squadron was disbanded at RAF Brüggen. (R.A.R. Carrey)

Sqn Ldr C.P. Starck flies 3 Squadron's Javelin FAW 4 (XA638) 'J' over the Netherlands. Like 87 Squadron at Brüggen, 3 Squadron was disbanded in early 1961, leaving just two all-weather fighter units in RAF Germany: 5 and 11 Squadrons. (3 Squadron)

of 3 Squadron commented that 'though interesting [*Flashback*] did not produce the expected number of night raids.'

Reflecting the experiments carried out within Fighter Command, Javelins of 87 Squadron attempted mixed interceptions with Hunters of 4 Squadron in October. A Javelin and a Hunter would operate as a pair, with the Hunter flying in close formation for the take-off, approach and landing. Once in the operating area the Javelin used its radar to vector the Hunter towards its target.

1961

Exercise *Flashback* was the last exercise undertaken by 87 and 3 Squadron Javelins: both units were disbanded in early January 1961, belated victims of the 1957 Defence White Paper. The immediate result of these disbandments was an influx of experienced Javelin crews into the remaining Javelin units in Germany: 11 Squadron inherited eight crews from 3 Squadron while 5 Squadron received a number of ex-87 Squadron crews. Thus RAF Germany started 1961 with its two Javelin squadrons manned by experienced crews, but still with a gun-armed fighter at a time when most of Fighter Command's fighter units were already armed with missiles. This shortcoming would become apparent during the Berlin crisis, which unfolded over the summer.

Aircrew from 3 Squadron pose in front of Javelin FAW 4 (XA762) 'B' at RAF Laarbruch in November 1959. The squadron was disbanded just over a year later and most of its crews were posted to the remaining RAFG Javelin units. (3 Squadron)

Javelin FAW 4s from 11 Squadron flying in echelon formation from RAF Geilenkirchen. In January 1961, the squadron received a large influx of aircrews from the recently-disbanded 3 Squadron. (Crown copyright)

Both Javelin squadrons carried out exchanges during the year. The first was between 5 Squadron and 337 Squadron RNoAF. Six Javelins visited Gardermoen in the last week of May and the reciprocal visit by six F-86Ks took place the following week. At the end of August, 11 Squadron had a simultaneous exchange with 445 Squadron RCAF (CF-100s) at Marville, France.

The Duncan Trophy

Just as Fighter Command held annual proficiency competitions such as the Ingen Trophy, so RAF Germany's fighter squadrons competed for the Duncan Trophy. During the 1950s, the trophy was awarded to the squadron achieving the highest average air-to-air gunnery score at APC. In 1959, the first year that Javelin squadrons competed, 87 and 3 Squadrons had come second and third respectively after Hunters of 26 Squadron. In 1960 it was decided that APC gunnery was too academic an exercise to be a measure of tactical proficiency; instead the competition was decided on ciné weave scores. In the 1960 competition, the first three places went to Hunter squadrons, but by the summer of 1961 there were only three fighter squadrons left in RAF Germany: 5 and 11 Squadron (Javelins) and 14 Squadron (Hunter F6 day fighters). This would also be the final year of APCs at Sylt as the base was due to close at the end of the year. The first

Javelin FAW 4s of 11 Squadron in 'Vic' formation. By early 1961, only two Javelin squadrons remained in RAF Germany, but it was already apparent that the gun-armed Javelins were obsolescent. (Crown copyright)

competitors, 14 Squadron, set a high score of 81.7 percent in May, but it was narrowly topped by 11 Squadron with an average of 81.9 percent the following month; however, in July 5 Squadron, squeezed ahead with a score of 82.6 percent to win the competition.

Berlin

The political tension over Berlin, which had been increasing over the summer months, broke into a full-blown crisis in August once the construction of the Berlin Wall commenced. In response, both of Fighter Command's Javelin FAW 8 squadrons were dispatched to reinforce RAF Germany: 41 Squadron arrived at Geilenkirchen on 11 August, to be followed by 85 Squadron at Laarbruch the following month. Both units were used to cover the increased Battle Flight commitment. For 41 Squadron the detachment got off to a bad start with a fatal accident. Flt Lt J.L. Hatch and Flt Lt J.C.P. Northall carried out a high-speed low-level break into the circuit at the end of a sortie on 29 August. At 460kts the elevators proved to be extremely effective, and generated a loading of 11g, well past the structural limit of the aircraft (FAW 8, XH971), which disintegrated.

Both pairs in the Battle Flight of 41 Squadron were scrambled on 8 September, and one pair was diverted to Gütersloh to take up Battle Flight duties there. Four more Javelins were sent to Gütersloh the next day, to bolster the enhanced Battle Flight. Over the next week from dawn to dusk one Javelin maintained two minutes' readiness in company with two Hunters from 14 Squadron; the second Javelin was at five minutes and the third at thirty minutes' readiness.

Meanwhile 5 and 11 Squadrons continued with 'business as usual:' both squadrons took part in the three-day Exercise *Checkmate* in mid-September. The exercise scenario provided a steady if unspectacular number of scrambles, but when they came, rapid scrambles of twelve aircraft at a time were the order of the day. Both squadrons ended up operating from RAF Wildenrath on the last day of the exercise after their home bases were 'exercise destroyed.' Later in the year, Exercise *Roulette* brought interceptions against CF-100s F-84s, F-101s, F-102s and F-104 Starfighters. Replacement of the Javelin FAW 4s on 11 Squadron with the slightly longer-range Javelin FAW 5s started in August, although it was not until February 1962 that the last FAW 4s left Geilenkirchen.

The arrangements put in place in summer 1961 continued through 1962: while Fighter Command's missile-armed Javelins covered the extra QRA commitment

An aerial view of the Javelin FAW 9s of 25 Squadron parked in revetments at RAF Gütersloh during the Berlin Crisis of 1962. Missile-armed Javelins from the UK took turns to hold alert in Germany for the duration of the crisis.

The tail markings on the two Javelins tell the story: a group of aircrew from 33 Squadron are about to rebadge themselves to become a new Javelin FAW 9-equipped 5 Squadron at RAF Geilenkirchen in December 1962. (33 Squadron)

from Gütersloh, Javelin squadrons in RAF Germany continued the 2 TAF routine. After Taceval in March, Geilenkirchen was temporarily closed in the early summer, so 11 Squadron moved to Brüggen for two months. This period also included a simultaneous exchange with the F-86Ks of 334 Squadron RNoAF based at Bodø. Meanwhile, 5 Squadron concentrated on lane control exercises each month from Laarbruch until May. In that month the squadron exchanged with 423 Squadron (RCAF), a CF-100 unit based at Grostenquin, to the northeast of Nancy, France

Twelve Javelins from 11 Squadron also deployed to Nicosia on 15 September 1962. Here they took advantage of the good weather to fly air-to-air gunnery sorties before joining in Exercise *Neocex* in the first week in October. The exercise flying was mostly at low-level from Akrotiri and the crews found it most enjoyable. The squadron returned to Geilenkirchen on 19 October, just in time for the station's Taceval ten days later.

The New Order

However, the days of the gun-armed Javelins were numbered and 5 and 11 squadrons were both disbanded as Javelin FAW 5 units in November and December 1962 respectively, to be simultaneously reformed at Geilenkirchen as Javelin FAW 9 units.

The nucleus of the 'new' 5 Squadron was provided by 33 Squadron and 25 Squadron's aircraft and crews formed the basis for the 'new' 11 Squadron. RAF Germany's new missile-armed Javelins took over Battle Flight at Geilenkirchen from mid-December. A new Battle Flight hut was completed in January 1963, so at least there was some warmth and shelter for the groundcrew as they waited at readiness.

The aircrew soon got used to their new operating environment, although perhaps inevitably there were a few close shaves as they settled in. On 23 January 1963, an 11 Squadron crew, Flt Sgt R.E. Kelly and Sgt R.G. Evans, was flying on a typically murky day. Evans recalled that they 'climbed to forty thousand feet looking for some "trade"... any other aircraft which we could engage. Soon we espied four F-84Fs slightly below us, so we "bounced" them, eventually getting behind a pair of them whilst the other pair tried to do the same to us. After a merry "circle of joy" lasting about five minutes, the "enemy" decide to break off and go home, leaving us with a rather empty sky. A quick Gee-fix put us sixty nautical miles north-northeast of base, with fuel of two thousand two hundred pounds each side, so in order to reach base with our "Bingo" fuel we elected to do a fuel-conserving "glide" on one engine at two-twenty knots... we continued the glide to flight level two-five-zero on our dive-circle... [and] descended on it to flight level one-five-zero then turned in intersect the extended centre line for runway two seven, continuing our descent to three thousand feet... To my great surprise, all GEE-signals disappeared at eight thousand feet, which was most unusual as normally we kept sight of them until we landed. I told Bob about this and we levelled off at four thousand feet just about our safety height. We tried to contact Geilenkirchen approach frequency... SILENCE. We again tried,

A mass launch by Javelin FAW 9s of 5 Squadron on a hazy day; the unit's Javelin T3 is in the left foreground, distinguishable by the pen-nib fairing over the jet pipes. (5 Squadron)

still silence. By now that little word all aviators dread came to mind… LOST. After about twenty minutes on a south-south-westerly heading, I reckoned we were in the south-west quadrant from base, and a check on the base ILS localizer indeed said we were south of an east/west line through Geilenkirchen. We called on the emergency frequency prefixing our call with "Mayday, Mayday, Mayday"… still no answer. I told Bob to turn onto a north-easterly heading and this is where my guardian angel came into play. My wife and I were living on the married quarters in Wildenrath and while we were having a social drink in the sergeants' mess one evening, I chanced to talk to a chief technician who told me that a new, superior aerial system had been installed at ATC to improve the CADAF [direction-finding equipment] performance. Our own CADAF at Geilenkirchen had been unserviceable for weeks, so I swiftly found the approach frequency for Wildenrath. Bob dialled this up, we called "Mayday" again and this time a very faint voice answered saying, "Aircraft calling steer zero-four-zero and repeat call sign." We complied of course, and all the time we were peering through the fog and mist to try to see the ground: no such luck… By this time I had turned up the "Gain" on my AI radar set and gained a negative response across our track which I hoped was the river Maas [Meuse], putting us approximately twenty-five miles from Wildenrath. We again called approach, they asked us to "squawk ident," and then they

A formal portrait of 5 Squadron personnel taken at RAF Geilenkirchen in April 1963. (5 Squadron)

said they could see an echo thirty miles away, on our heading… it had to be us, no other aircraft was to be seen. We slowly descended to two thousand feet to intercept the ILS glideslope for runway zero nine. Down we went and after three long minutes Bob said he had the approach lights dead ahead. We landed after a sortie length of one hour twenty-five minutes, when we normally only flew for one hour.'

A more serious incident occurred during an air-combat sortie on 6 May: an 11 Squadron Javelin (FAW 9, XH884) flown by Flt Lt N.J. Glass was attempting to achieve a firing solution on its target when the aircraft flicked and entered a spin. The navigator, Fg Off A. Evans, ejected at 19,000ft, but Glass regained control at 14,000ft and was able to recover the aircraft to Geilenkirchen.

Although Battle Flight was routinely maintained at Geilenkirchen, Javelins were frequently deployed further east to reduce the transit time to the ADIZ. In February, 11 Squadron took part in Exercise *Quicksand II*, operating from Celle for the last week of the month. In April, 5 Squadron provided two aircraft each day to stand alert duty from Gütersloh. The squadron also provided six aircraft for

Checking the flag for hits: Javelin crews of 5 Squadron during the APC at RNLAF Leeuwarden in July 1963. (5 Squadron)

Quicksand III in June. Another six Javelins from 5 Squadron staged to Bodø via Aalborg and Oerland on 2 June. The weather was not particularly good and the mountains were looming out of the clouds as they arrived, but the aircraft still managed five sorties while they were in Norway.

APC and MPCs

The closure of Sylt meant that another venue was needed for APCs. Both the Hunters of 14 Squadron and the Javelins of 11 Squadron had used Cyprus in 1962, but in 1963, the RNAF base at Leeuwarden and the Dutch ranges over the Friesian islands were chosen for both Javelin squadrons. In June 1963, 11 Squadron flew the first APC, followed the next month by 5 Squadron.

In late 1965, both Javelin squadrons in RAF Germany were allocated a number of missiles to fire at MPC from Valley. Once again, the first squadron to deploy from Germany was 11 Squadron, in the last week of September. Unfortunately it was too windy to fire, but 5 Squadron managed to fire all five of their missiles the following month.

Exercises

Taceval for Geilenkirchen and the RAF Germany Javelin force was on 22 October, after which there was a relatively quiet period for both squadrons over the winter months. The first exercise commitment of 1964 was Exercise *Quicksand*, the deployment to Celle in support of the Berlin air corridors. Javelins from both 5 and 11 Squadrons flew from Celle during much of March. For 11 Squadron there was an opportunity to join an army co-operation exercise, giving crews the chance for some low flying as they carried out simulated attacks against ground targets. The squadron also carried out an exchange with 3/30 Squadron of the French Air Force, a Vautour-equipped unit based at Rheims.

The first of what was to become an annual NATO exercise, *Sky Blue*, was held on 6 May and 5 Squadron flew twelve sorties on this exercise. However, the following month heralded the much larger Exercise *Northern Express*, a major air, land and sea exercise to practise the reinforcement of NATO's northern flank and operations in Norway and the Norwegian Sea. Eight Javelins from 11 Squadron, led by Sqn Ldr P. Deakin and four Javelins from 5 Squadron deployed to Bodø.

A dramatic view of two Javelin FAW 9s (XH713) 'B' and (XH756) 'Z' from 5 Squadron.
(5 Squadron)

Javelin FAW 9 (XH912) 'S' from 5 Squadron scrambles from 'battle flight' in 1963.
(5 Squadron)

A 'Box Four' formation of Javelin FAW 9s from 5 Squadron in September 1963: Sqn Ldr Hamlin and Fg Off Joe Sim lead with Tim Carter and Roy Martin on the right, with Rex Boulton and Harry Barker on the left. Reg Hallam and Tony Bradley fly in the 'Number 4' slot. (5 Squadron)

Here they joined Norwegian units as well as USAF F-100 and F-101 squadrons. Each aircraft flew some twelve exercise sorties, mostly at high-level, but there were not many targets for the Javelins to engage. Later in the month 11 Squadron, operating from Geilenkirchen, flew sixty-two sorties on Exercise *Co-Op 64*. The exercise scenario was divided into a low-level phase in the mornings and high-level phase in the afternoon.

In a busy two months, 5 Squadron returned to Bodø with six Javelins led by Sqn Ldr Taylor in August and it sent another six Javelins to Malta to be part of a thirty-aircraft flypast on 21 September celebrating Malta's independence. Meanwhile, 11 Squadron's APC took place at Leeuwarden in August. Then, in response to increased activity on the eastern side of the Inner German Border, seven Javelins were sent to Gütersloh to mount forward QRA over 24 and 25 September. Both squadrons also carried out successful MPCs in October.

Low-Level Flying

On 1 October 1964, the role of the Javelin in RAF Germany officially became that of low-level air defence. Although both squadrons made serious attempts to practise their new role, they were to some extent thwarted by the weather and with the closure of the Low Flying Areas (LFA) because of migrating birds. As Wg Cdr W.J. Marriott, OC 11 Squadron wrote: 'It is unfortunate that the squadron has to assume its new role at this time of the year when the weather is frequently unsuitable for this form of flying.' In view of the poor weather at low-level, 11 Squadron concentrated instead on flying four-ship formations at high-level, with the emphasis on missile battle formation and two-versus-two air combat. It was not really until the summer of 1965 that either Javelin unit was able to get to grips fully with the low-level role.

The first few months of 1965 proved to be another busy time for the Javelins of 5 Squadron. Six aircraft deployed once more to Bodø on 9 February for a ten-day detachment. This included a pair sent to Bardufoss to standby at ten-minutes readiness. The aircraft were scrambled during the night, for what was probably the first operational Javelin sortie in the Arctic Circle. At the beginning of April there was another crisis over Berlin. Soviet and East German forces attempted to close the air corridors in order to prevent an extraordinary meeting of the *Bundestag* from taking place in Berlin. Supreme Headquarters Allied Powers Europe (SHAPE) initiated Operation *Gopherwood* on 6 April which involved British, US and French forces keeping the corridors open. For the RAF this meant flying Armstrong-Whitworth Argosy transport aircraft along the corridors and the deployment at very short notice of five Javelins from 5 Squadron to Celle to maintain QRA.

However, events were already overtaking 5 Squadron. In March, the unit was required to provide 7½ crews to leave for Singapore as soon as possible and it was a much-reduced squadron which carried out a successful MPC at Valley in June. In July, six Javelins from 5 Squadron flew to Cameri (west of Milan) for a final exchange with 21° Gruppo Italian Air Force, an F-104 Starfighter unit. In September, after the arrival of the Lightnings of 19 Squadron at Gütersloh, 5 Squadron was disbanded.

A formation of RAF Geilenkirchen-based aircraft [11 Squadron Javelin FAW 9s and a 3 Squadron Canberra B(I)8] for the visit of HRH the Duke of Edinburgh in December 1964. (11 Squadron)

Meanwhile, 11 Squadron had spent much of the summer practising the low-level air-defence role both at day and night. Night tactics were trialled in July, to work out how a pair of aircraft could work together at low-level in darkness. The system was for one aircraft to perform the intercept to identify the target, while the other covered the interceptor from a safe distance but within missile range. The squadron aircraft took to flying in three-aircraft sections at night, with one aircraft acting as target for the other pair. 'Most crews were surprised at the relative ease with which this could be done,' recorded Flt Lt J.D. Rust.

There was a brief return to high-level work during the year's Exercise *Sky Blue*, which took place in August. The squadron absorbed some of the personnel from 5 Squadron when the unit disbanded, but their reprieve was short-lived. Like 5 Squadron, the last major event for 11 Squadron was a simultaneous exchange, this time with 724 Squadron RDAF from Skrydstrup in September. In January 1966, 11 Squadron disbanded.

seven

FAR EAST
1961 - 1968

Heartfelt Words

Flt Lt J.D. Hutchinson's words were undoubtedly heartfelt when he wrote of the Singapore *Adex* in August 1961 that, 'crews were able to demonstrate for the first time in this theatre the vast superiority of performance of their fighter over the Canberra which has had the edge for so long.' After soldiering on with their obsolete Meteor NF-14s, 60 Squadron finally saw its first Javelin FAW 9s arrive at Tengah in July 1961. 'The undoubted highlight of the month was the arrival of five intact Javelins,' wrote Hutchinson, adding that, 'morale rose almost visibly.' It had been a long wait for the squadron, which was the last dedicated night-fighter squadron in the RAF to re-equip with the Javelin. Crews had been detached to 228 OCU in January 1961 for conversion courses in anticipation of the new aircraft, but it was not until 10:20hrs on 26 July that the squadron commander, Wg Cdr P. Smith, MBE and Flt Lt J.W. Betts flew the first Javelin in 60 Squadron markings.

One of the biggest challenges in re-equipping a unit in the Far East was the logistics in getting all of the aircraft there. Although Exercise *Dyke* had proved the viability of using an AAR trail to deploy Javelins to Singapore, Exercises *Pounce* and *Canterlup* had not yet demonstrated the practicality of moving an entire squadron's worth of aircraft in this way. Instead it was decided to stage the aircraft in three batches of four to six, using experienced Javelin crews from Fighter Command squadrons to fly the aircraft. Each deployment took around two weeks, as the aircraft negotiated their way along a route which went from Waterbeach via Istres, Luqa, El Adem, Diyabakir, Tehran, Bahrain, Sharjah, Masirah, Karachi, New Delhi, Benares, Calcutta, Rangoon, Bangkok and Butterworth to Tengah. The first ferry flight went well and delivered the five Javelins which arrived in July. The second

The flight line at RAF Tengah, Singapore, with Javelin FAW 9 (XH964) 'T' of 60 Squadron in the foreground. (J Abell)

flight was less successful, losing one Javelin to a refuelling accident in Malta and another to a fatal accident over the Ganges Delta on 5 August. That aircraft (FAW 9, XH791) had broken up after flying into a cumulo-nimbus cloud and suffering from centre-line closure. The pilot, Flt Lt E.N. Owens, was killed during his ejection, which may well have been inadvertent; the navigator, Master Nav A.D. Melton ejected successfully but then spent three days in the jungle before he was rescued. The four surviving Javelins arrived at Tengah on 8 August.

By September, the squadron had twelve Javelins and was playing a full part in the monthly *Adexes* and *Bomexes*. In October the squadron exercised with naval aircraft from HMS *Victorious* (R38), flying PIs against de Havilland Sea Vixens and Supermarine Scimitars. Both air-to-air and air-to-ground gunnery sorties were also flown, the latter using the range at China Rock as a target. Routine training sorties mainly comprised PIs, both at low and high level. Many of these were flown as pairs, with each Javelin taking turns to fly as fighter and target, but the many other aircraft based in Singapore – the resident Canberras and Hunters, as well as the myriad of visiting types – also provided targets for interceptions.

The squadron benefitted from a visit by AWFCS in February 1962 and the following month they were able to apply some of the lessons when Wg Cdr Smith led four Javelins to Butterworth for a five-day detachment. Here they flew air combat sorties against Commonwealth Aircraft Corporation CA-27 Sabres of 77 Squadron (RAAF). The Javelins acquitted themselves against the Sabres surprisingly well. In March, the squadron was working with the Royal Navy

Javelin FAW 9 (XH725) 'P' of 60 Squadron climbs away: The squadron's makhor head badge is painted on the tail, with silver and black stripes above. (M.H. Miller)

once again, this time with HMS *Ark Royal*. Exercise *Fantail* was planned to run from 25 to 27 April. On the first day the Javelins attacked the carrier and that night they defended Singapore, using Fairey Gannet AEW 3s of 849C Naval Air Squadron (NAS) to provide intercept control, against attacks by Sea Vixens from HMS *Ark Royal*. Unfortunately, the rest of the exercise was cancelled because of poor weather.

Indonesian Tu-16s

Headquarters Far East Air Force (FEAF) instructed 60 Squadron to come to fifteen minutes' readiness from 23 May because of the presence of three Soviet-built Tupolev Tu-16KS (Badger) aircraft and their AS-1 air-to-surface missiles at Medan on Northern Sumatra. They were on delivery to the *Tentara Nasional Indonesia-Angakatan Udara* (TNI-AU – Indonesian Air Force) and were the first Tu-16s to be exported outside the Soviet Union. Two Javelins (FAW 9, XH722 [Flt Lts J.H. Adams/T.P. Burns] and FAW 9, XH835 [Flt Lt B.J. O'Donovan/Mstr Nav D.J. Glenross]) had been diverted to Butterworth and they were scrambled on 29 May when the Tu-16s took off. However, they remained inside Indonesian airspace and could not be intercepted. Another delivery was due later in June and once again the Javelins of 60 Squadron waited at readiness. This time they were successful in finding and photographing five Tu-16s. Wg Cdr Smith with Sqn Ldr F.S.W. Jolliffe intercepted three Tu-16s, while Fg Offs D. Haywood and J. Andrews found another two.

Another view of Javelin FAW 9 (XH725) 'P', this time with a Firestreak missile mounted on the outboard pylon. (M.H. Miller)

HMS *Ark Royal* called in at Singapore again in July, enabling 60 Squadron to work with her air contingent once more and in the early autumn twelve Javelins deployed to Butterworth to participate in the air-defence Exercise *John Collins*, which took place from 18 to 26 September. Exercise *Charlton*, at the end of November was an electronic warfare exercise in which the targets were Electronic Counter Measures (ECM) Valiants. On the morning of 3 December, Wg Cdr Smith and Sqn Ldr Jolliffe led a pair of Javelins in a 'snake' climb through thick cloud to carry out PIs with one of the ECM Valiants. Climbing through 36,000ft, Jolliffe reported: 'There was a tremendous explosion and the aircraft (FAW 9, XH836) pitched violently nose down.' Jolliffe ejected successfully and Smith found himself in an inverted spin with no response from the elevators or ailerons. He, too, ejected and was picked up a little later by a Bristol Belvedere helicopter. Despite an extensive air search, it was not until two days later that Jolliffe was found alive and well by a Gurkha patrol. The aircraft had suffered a catastrophic centre-line closure.

The Beginnings of Confrontation

After the unsuccessful revolt in Brunei in December 1962, the Indonesian government announced its policy of 'Confrontation' in January 1963. At Tengah a twenty-four hour QRA, nicknamed Operation *Tramp*, was established, with two live-armed Javelins kept at thirty minutes readiness. In practice this did not affect routine flying by 60 Squadron, which continued through the year. Wg Cdr Smith

A spectacular view of Javelin FAW 9 (XH846) 'F' from 60 Squadron as it flies along the Singapore waterfront at low-level. The letters 'JF' on the tail are the initials of the commanding officer, Wg Cdr J. 'Jock' Fraser. (C.J. Donovan)

handed command of the squadron to Wg Cdr J. Fraser in April, giving his successor time to settle in before the major exercises started in the late summer. Six Javelins were detached to Butterworth for the *Adex* in August and Exercise *Fotex* took place in the South China Sea from 2 to 8 August. During *Fotex* the Javelins acted alternately as bombers and fighters. In the former role they carried out strikes on the ships and were able to strafe splash targets towed by some warships; in the latter they defended Singapore against attacks by FAA Sea Vixens.

However, increased political tension in September resulted in the *Tramp* commitment to be increased to six aircraft at Tengah. One of the *Tramp* aircraft (FAW 9, XH721) had been scrambled on the night of 17 October: Flt Lt L.G. Buckingham and Flt Lt A.J. Cleverley intercepted an unlit contact flying in international airspace over the Malacca Straits. They were able to identify their target as an TNI-AU Tu-16. From 21 October, the 'Tramp state' was raised further to include two Javelins at two minutes' readiness from Butterworth. This was later relaxed to five minutes' readiness from dusk to dawn, with Sabres of 77 Squadron Royal Australian Air Force (RAAF) covering the daylight hours. As the international situation deteriorated further in November, four aircraft and crews of 64 Squadron were diverted from detachment in India to reinforce the Javelin strength in Singapore and Malaya. One of the defining characteristics of the Confrontation period from the perspective of the Javelin units was the vast distances (and land areas) that had to be patrolled and defended: Butterworth was over 300 nautical miles northwest of Singapore, with all the complications of command and control that distance brought.

Operating from Tengah, Javelin FAW 9 (XH964) 'T' is part of a 60 Squadron patrol over the fish traps in the Malacca Straits. (J. Abell)

Exercises and training continued through November and December. Nine Javelins deployed to Butterworth for Exercise *John Collins IV* in November. While they were there they took the opportunity to investigate whether the Firestreak acquisition head could track rockets fired from the Sabres. The purpose of this experiment was to see if it might be possible to use the rockets as targets for live Firestreak firings at a later date. A trial was also flown against a Vickers Valetta to investigate whether the Firestreak could acquire a lock on against a piston-engined aircraft as it would be useful to know if the missile could be used, if necessary, against North American P-51 Mustangs and Douglas B-25 Mitchells of the TNI-AU.

In another trial of possible tactics against low-flying Indonesian aircraft, Exercise *Kit Kat* had Javelin-Hunter pairs flying race-track patrol patterns to the east of China Rock, defending against Sea Vixens and Buccaneers from HMS *Victorious* as well as Canberras from Tengah.

Operational Detachments

By the end of 1963, it was clear that RAF fighters would also be needed to support operations over Borneo and that more Javelins would be required to cover the massive areas of mainland Malaya and Singapore, as well as Borneo. The solution was the permanent establishment at Butterworth of a new 'C' Flight. This was to be commanded by Sqn Ldr J.G. Ince, who arrived in Malaya at the head of another four Javelins and crews from 23 Squadron, during Operation *Merino*, in January 1964. Ince's arrival brought the total number of aircraft at Butterworth to eight; it also brought the first Javelin FAW 9Rs to the Far East, providing at least a nucleus of longer-range aircraft.

Despite an official ceasefire, the Indonesians declared their intention to supply guerrilla forces in Borneo by air. As a result, the boundaries of Sarawak and Sabah were declared an ADIZ from 00:30hrs on 25 February. The previous day the commanding officer of 60 Squadron had led two Javelins (plus a detachment of Hunters from 20 Squadron) to Kuching (almost 400 nautical miles east of Singapore) and four more Javelins were established at RAF Labuan (a further 360 nautical miles distant). A mobile radar unit was also deployed to Labuan. Fighters were maintained at readiness at Kuching and Labuan, but low-level standing patrols were also routinely flown along the borders, as were close escort sorties for the RAF and Royal New Zealand Air Force (RNZAF) transport aircraft carrying out supply drops. The flying conditions were challenging: the operating area was a vast and generally poorly-mapped jungle which included mountains rising above 13,000ft. Furthermore, much of the high terrain was frequently obscured in low cloud or heavy rain showers.

At the end of February 1964, 60 Squadron was stretched over a 1,000-mile front, maintaining QRA with two Javelins at Labuan, two at Kuching, four at Tengah and a further two at Butterworth. Although more reinforcement crews and aircraft arrived from the UK in March as part of Operation *Helen*, the squadron's personnel were stretched, too. As Wg Cdr Fraser pointed out: 'The maintenance of the detachments at Kuching and Labuan is a severe drain on the technical resources at base. Overtime

In January 1964, Sqn Ldr J.G. Ince led Operation Merino, *the reinforcement of the Far East by four Javelin FAW 9Rs of 23 Squadron. 'Chaz' Ince retired from the RAF in 1972.* (M.H. Miller)

A Vickers Valetta transport aircraft of 52 Squadron landing at RAF Kuching in December 1964 is framed between two Javelin FAW 9s of 60 Squadron. Much of the operational flying over Borneo by Javelins involved escorting transport aircraft to and from drop zones in the jungle. (J. Abell)

A pair of Javelin FAW 9s from 60 Squadron become airborne from RAF Kuching. (M.H. Miller)

A Javelin FAW 9 of 60 Squadron is silhouetted against the dusk as it banks over Sarawak in late 1964/early 1965. (J. Abell)

Javelin FAW 9 (XH841) 'D' of 60 Squadron at readiness on the ORP at RAF Kuching. Parked in the background is a Bristol Belvedere, twin-rotor helicopter from 66 Squadron. (J. Abell)

A pair of Javelin FAW 9s from 60 Squadron take-off for a supply drop escort sortie from RAF Kuching, late 1964 or early 1965. (J. Abell)

for the men has become the rule rather than the exception… the Javelin is not the aircraft for operating away from base without considerable technical backing.'

On 11 March, Operation *Franciscan*, a contingency plan for the low-level air defence of the island was initiated and all available aircraft were swiftly armed and brought up to readiness for immediate launch. It was only once the crews were 'on state' with engines running that they learnt that it was only a practice. Indonesian activity intensified in Borneo over April and while escorting a supply drop one Javelin was fired on by a 12.5mm anti-aircraft gun. Intelligence received later via radio intercepts indicated that sixty rounds had been fired, although none of them had hit the aircraft. A month later, a Javelin (FAW 9, XH876), flown by Fg Offs D.W. Barden and G.M. Warden was hit by ground fire and after landing at Kuching a hole (made by a light-calibre bullet) was discovered in the engine intake.

Earlier, on 16 May, two Javelins from the Kuching detachment had helped to capture a launch near Lundu, just to the west of Kuching. The launch refused to comply with instructions from a patrol vessel to stop and back up was requested from the RAF. In short time, two Javelins (FAW 9R, XH887 [Flt Lts K.F. Scott/W.G. Fullilove] and FAW 9R, XH766 [Plt Off B Todd/Flt Lt G.T. Hall]) appeared on the scene and conducted such an impressive low-level beat-up that the launch immediately surrendered and was later boarded by crew from the minesweeper HMS *Wilkieston* (M1192).

At this time Operation *Tramp* was expanded to include daily dawn and dusk patrols along the Malayan coast and the Borneo detachments were each expanded to three aircraft and four crews. The Javelin FAW 9Rs tended to be used for the Borneo detachments as in the two-tank, two-missile fit they could fly 1¾ hour patrols at low-level. Personnel were rotated between Singapore and Borneo at fortnightly intervals. Over the summer months, the Javelin force (60 Squadron now included crews and aircraft seconded from 23 and 64 Squadrons, as well as its own) at Singapore carried out numerous border patrols and transport escorts. However, despite the increased tempo of operations some of the aircrew found opportunities for 'extra-curricular' activities, flying as second pilots in Westland Whirlwind HAR 10 helicopters in 225 Squadron. On one such sortie Flt Lt K.A. Pye brought back the bodies of five Indonesian soldiers who had been part of a fifty-strong force which had attacked a fortified village two miles from the Indonesian border on 31 July.

In another development, rioting broke out in Singapore and Flt Lt S.H. Davies found himself in command of thirty airmen who had been detailed to guard the radio transmitter station at Jurong. The situation in Singapore deteriorated further on 4 September when Indonesian paratroopers were dropped on the Malayan mainland near Labis. RAF Tengah was immediately put onto a war footing: all leave was cancelled, anti-aircraft guns were brought to readiness and station installations were fortified

Groundcrews from 60 Squadron at RAF Kuching, poring over servicing manuals before carrying out rectification work on a Javelin FAW 9. The high-serviceability rate of the Javelins on operations was a testament to the efforts of the groundcrews. (J. Abell)

Javelin FAW 9 (XH725) 'P' from 60 Squadron flying at low-level over Shell Island, Singapore: From mid-1964, patrols along the Malayan coast were flown at dawn and dusk on a daily basis. (J. Abell)

Javelin role equipment on display at RAF Tengah: Firestreak missiles are under the pylons ready-to-load and a set of ventral tanks are on either side of the nose of Javelin FAW 9 (XH777) 'R' from 60 Squadron. (M.H. Miller)

A 60 Squadron Javelin FAW 9 at low-level over the Sarawak jungle: Finding a target both in the air or on the ground depended on the crew making a visual contact – so sorties were flown at low altitude to see a ground target or to spot an aircraft against the skyline. (M.H. Miller)

with sandbags. From 12 September, 60 Squadron was operating from its wartime dispersals. Soon afterwards Operation *Colastine* provided reinforcements in the shape of 'A' Flight 64 Squadron whose eight Javelin FAW 9Rs were immediately put on alert: during daylight one Javelin was held at fifteen minutes' readiness, while in the hours of darkness this commitment was increased to include a further four Javelins at five minutes. Two more aircraft from 64 Squadron were sent to Butterworth.

After a busy summer, the situation seemed to be calming slightly in early October, but it soon flared up again. Another Javelin (FAW 9R, XH896) was hit by ground fire during a low-level patrol over Borneo on 16 October, but Flt Lt M.C. Gray and Flt Lt P.A. Bass were uninjured and the damage to the aircraft was superficial. The following month the alert state increased further at Tengah and standing patrols were flown at night in the Kuala Lumpur area. Incursions into Sarawak and Sabah by Indonesian irregulars also continued. On 10 December, a patrol from 1st Battalion 2nd King Edwards VII's Own Gurkhas was ambushed in the jungle by a force of some 100 guerrilla fighters. In a critical situation, they called for air support and Flt Lt R.E. Lockhart and Flt Lt S.H. Davies, who were on a routine patrol from Labuan (FAW 9R, XH908), diverted to the scene. Unable to use the guns, Lockhart instead continuously 'buzzed' the Indonesian positions at low-level, selecting reheat as he passed overhead. The Javelin reheats lit with a 'bang', which led the Indonesians to believe that they were being bombed. This in turn meant that their attack faltered and they withdrew.

Training Continues

Despite all the operational work, the Javelin crews at Tengah, comprising 'A' and 'B' Flights of 60 Squadron and 'A' Flight of 64 Squadron, continued with routine training. During Exercise *Irongate*, held in January 1965, they flew against Canberras and Victors, and 64 Squadron's crews also carried out AAR, as well as low-level PIs with FAA Scimitars. Both units also practised air-to-air gunnery, but the disappointing average of 5.3 percent achieved by 60 Squadron was as much a reflection on the lack of practice during the previous year's operations as it was of the lack of harmonization on the battle-weary Javelins. On 27 March, Exercise *Showpiece* was a fifteen-aircraft formation flypast around Singapore by 60 Squadron as a formal show of strength.

Meanwhile, operations over Borneo continued and the 1,000th operational sortie over the island was flown by Flt Lt J.S.C. Davis and Lt R. Patterson, RN, (FAW 9R, XH959) on 29 March. There were two incursions into Sarawak in April. The first, to the south of Tebedu, took place on 15 April. Flt Lt W.W. Hill and Flt Lt D.R. Octon were called to give air support to ground troops. Unfortunately they were unable to do so, but they were able to act as a radio relay and pass information to a section of ground attack Hunters. Two weeks later 2nd Battalion, Parachute Regiment, was attacked and outnumbered by a large force near Pang Amo (close to the border, south of Kuching). Although the two Javelins (FAW 9R, XH877 [Flt Lts J.B. Abell/S.H. Davies] and FAW 9R, XH885 [Fg Off R.D. Browne/Flt Lt R. Houghton]) did not intervene directly, they escorted Hastings and Valetta transport aircraft as they dropped supplies to support the paratroopers.

The extra range and loiter time of the Javelin FAW 9R made it better suited to operations over Borneo. A tired looking FAW 9R (XH908) 'S' in 60 Squadron colours is at readiness at RAF Labuan in 1965.
(I. Alder)

Back at Tengah Flt Sgt L.F. Faulkner and Flt Lt A.J. Cleverley were launched (FAW 9, XH777) from *Tramp* at 08:20hrs on 17 April to intercept an unidentified contact approaching from the east. Still over international waters, they rolled out behind an Tu-16 of the TNI-AU, which then turned away.

64 Squadron

After six months of operating as two Flights split between Binbrook and Tengah, 64 Squadron was formally reformed at Tengah on 1 April 1965. However, it was almost immediately spilt into two parts once again the following month, with one flight responsible for the air defence of Singapore and the Malay Peninsula and the other covering the Borneo detachment. Responsibility for operations over Borneo passed from 60 Squadron to 64 Squadron in May. During this month there were also two *Tramp* scrambles from Tengah by 64 Squadron crews who intercepted Indonesian Tu-16s.

The first Javelin loss over Borneo occurred on 22 June 1965. Flt Lt P.J. Hart and Flt Lt P.E. Dell (FAW 9R, XH877) were on a routine low-level patrol near Tawau on the eastern coast of Sabah, when they saw an unidentified aircraft, which they went to intercept. On closing with the contact they were able to identify it as a Malayan Airways Douglas DC3 airliner, which was flying slowly, and the crew closed towards it with the engines of the Javelin at idle power. When Hart opened the throttles to accelerate away, the port engine exploded and the aircraft became uncontrollable. Both crew ejected successfully and were rescued. Another Javelin

Javelin FAW 9R (XH959) 'U' from 60 Squadron, flown by Flt D.W. Warne and Fg Off J.S. Thomson, accompanies a Hawker-Siddeley Argosy transport aircraft of 215 Squadron during a supply drop escort mission from RAF Kuching on 3 June 1964. (RAF Museum)

(FAW 9R, XH759) of 64 Squadron was severely damaged on 4 July when two 30mm rounds exploded in the ammunition bay in the wing while the aircraft was on patrol. Flt Lt M.C. Gray and Flt Lt W.D.G. Blundell recovered to Kuching, but three more rounds exploded after landing.

The Borneo commitment represented approximately 75 percent of 64 Squadron's total flying; a total, in September, of 179 sorties. One frustration for crews in Borneo was the lack of adequate warning, which sometimes prevented interception of Indonesian aircraft on the Malaysian side of the border with Kalimantan. In September, a Javelin on a low-level patrol unexpectedly met an TNI-AU Lockheed C-130 Hercules head-on in a valley close to the border, but before the Javelin could attack the Hercules made a 'violent turn' and re-crossed the border. The Borneo operations wound down in October and 8 October the Javelins of 64 Squadron were withdrawn from Borneo. However, there remained a commitment to redeploy two aircraft each to Kuching and Labuan at twelve hours' notice.

Indonesian Tu-16s were intercepted regularly from Tengah. On 26 June a 60 Squadron crew, Flt Lt D.W. Barden and Fg Off G.M. Warden, scrambled (FAW 9, XH777) from *Tramp* at 21:00hrs and intercepted a Tu-16 which carried no markings. In subsequent months it was the turn of 64 Squadron: Flt Lt J.E. Dellow and Flt Lt J.W. Jackson launched (FAW 9, XH841) from *Tramp* at 10:15hrs on 30 August and shadowed an TNI-AU Tu-16 along the international border in the middle of the Malacca Straits. On 21 September, Flt Lt C.V. Holman and Flt Lt B. Baranowski were diverted from a routine training sortie to shadow another TNI-AU Tu-16 in the Malacca Straits.

Missile Practice

In April 1965, the Butterworth flight had unsuccessfully attempted to fire Firestreak missiles at rockets fired by Sabres of 77 Squadron (RAAF). A different technique was tried in September, using 4.5-inch flares dropped by a Canberra. However, this method had some drawbacks, because as Wg Cdr Miller, pointed out: 'this was a severe test for the Firestreak, since the slowly descending stationary target was outside its designed parameters, yet a one hundred percent success rate was achieved.' On 14 and 15 September, two missiles were fired successfully by Javelins flying at 5,000ft and 300kt. The first Firestreak was fired by Flt Lt R.E. Lockhart and Flt Lt I.J. Cooper (FAW 9, XH846) and the second by Flt Lt W.W. Hill and Flt Lt D.R. Octon, (FAW 9, XH956). Three months later, 64 Squadron crews fired five Firestreaks in the same way. During Exercise *Conger Eel* in January, 60 Squadron crews fired more missiles at flares dropped by Canberras from 45 Squadron. The squadron also deployed Javelins and Meteor target tugs to Butterworth for air-to-air gunnery. More Firestreaks were fired at Butterworth in March.

The storm clouds are building as Javelin FAW 9 (XH777) 'R' from 60 Squadron takes off from RAF Kuching. Weather conditions could make flying very challenging over the poorly-mapped jungles of inland Borneo, especially when low cloud obscured the high ground. (J. Abell)

Restrictions on the Sapphire engines were introduced in July 1965. Initially non-operational flying was limited to flights above 10,000ft, which effectively stopped Javelin crews from practising low-level PIs. Later the restriction was lifted, but prolonged operation of the engines in the range 86 to 93 percent was then prohibited. Unfortunately this was the typical power setting for low-level cruise, so pilots resorted to the technique of flying with one engine at idle and the other at a higher power setting.

Two Javelins from 64 Squadron were lost on the night of 8 November. The first (FAW 9R, XH887) flown by Flt Lt K.E. Fitchew and Flt Lt A. Evans, was recovering from a routine night PI sortie but, when Fitchew selected the undercarriage down it did not lower. 'Because I had been a Javelin simulator instructor,' recalls Fitchew, 'the actions we were required to carry out were second nature to me. But because of my knowledge of the aircraft, I knew immediately that the undercarriage could not be lowered no matter what we did.' After going through the various checklists, the only option remaining was to eject from the aircraft. Although it was a 'controlled ejection,' Fitchew found that, 'what followed was without a doubt the most violent experience of my life, before or since. The effect on the occupant of the explosive charge needed to eject the seat is like, I imagine, being kicked by a mule. This was followed by the effect of the slipstream, which would be the same as, say, a hurricane with a strength of one hundred and eighty miles-per-hour; this being followed by violent tumbling, and somewhere in all this, I remember seeing the red glow of the Javelin's twin jet pipes going away from me into the distance.'

After landing in the sea, Fitchew was in his dinghy waiting to be rescued when: 'Suddenly and with little warning, I heard the roar of jet engines and a Javelin flew

After an extended period of being split between the UK and Singapore, 64 Squadron was reformed at RAF Tengah in June 1965. On the tail of Javelin FAW 9R (XH834) 'W' are the initials of the commanding officer, Wg Cdr P.D. Wright. (T. Evans)

A 64 Squadron 'see-off' crew helps the aircrew to strap into their Javelin on the line at RAF Tengah. Equipped with the longer-range Javelin FAW 9R, the squadron took responsibility for most of the Borneo operation. (T. Evans)

Firestreak missiles loaded onto a Javelin FAW 9 from 60 Squadron at RAF Kuching. MPCs were held at Butterworth where the missiles were fired against flares dropped by Canberra aircraft. (J. Abell)

A pair of 64 Squadron Javelin FAW 9Rs: XH961 'H' was the last Javelin to be damaged in an accident. On 8 February 1968, it suffered brake failure and left the runway on landing at RAF Tengah and hit a storm ditch. (T. Evans)

A 64 Squadron Javelin FAW 9R takes off from RAF Tengah; a Boeing HC-97G search and rescue aircraft of the USAF is in the foreground. (T. Evans)

very low over me from behind with its wheels down and landing lights on.' It seems that Flt Lt P.J. Poppe had decided to join the rescue operation and was trying to help to locate the survivors. 'It then climbed away,' continued Fitchew, 'and I assumed it would be returning to base. This was not the case. A few minutes later, I heard a roar of what sounded like a high-powered launch. I looked to the right, and in the distance saw what appeared to be the bow wave of a boat travelling at speed. The roar stopped suddenly and the bow wave subsided. All was silent except for what sounded like two small explosions. I knew immediately that an aircraft had flown into the sea.' The second Javelin (FAW 9R, XH959) had indeed flown into the sea, killing Poppe; fortunately his navigator, Flt Lt B.G.W. Unsted, survived after ejecting under water.

On 24 December 1965, with aircraft and crews withdrawn from Borneo and Butterworth, all of 64 Squadron's aircraft were now at Tengah – the first time since October 1963 that the squadron had been together on one station.

Continued Operations

Although Javelin operations in Borneo had largely ceased in January, the Confrontation was not yet over. At the beginning of February, 64 Squadron and its Javelins were back in Borneo. Later in the month, 60 Squadron, now commanded by Wg Cdr M.H. Miller, sent a fourship of Javelins to Kuching to assist. On 17 February, just after they had arrived in Borneo, Flt Lt C.V. Holman and Sqn Ldr G. Moores were scrambled (FAW 9, XH777) to assist in locating a guerrilla force, which was attempting to infiltrate to the south of Kuching. As they flew over a small jungle clearing in the search area, Moores spotted movement and Holman spent the next thirty minutes carrying out low-level 'beat-ups' of the area, using the

*Javelin FAW 9R (XH834) 'W' carries the initials of the commanding officer of 64
Squadron. A single Firestreak is carried on the outboard pylon.* (Tony O'Toole)

reheat in the same way that Flt Lt Lockhart had done just over a year previously.
The guerrillas were pinned down in this way until a patrol from 2nd Battalion, 7th
Gurkha Rifles was able to engage them, killing one and capturing the other five.
Unfortunately, Holman himself became a casualty when he fell down the steps of
the operations caravan after the sortie and broke his leg.

Apart from touring Sarawak as a 'flag waving' exercise, the aircraft resumed
the border patrols of the previous year. At the end of the month the Javelins were
withdrawn once again. However, at Tengah and Butterworth the *Tramp* state was
maintained and incidents continued to occur. On 21 April Fg Off Browne and Flt Lt
Woodward were scrambled from Butterworth to intercept an TNI–AU Ilyushin Il-
18 (reporting name Coot) transport aircraft. Then on 30 June 1966, two Javelins (Flt
Lts J.W.W. Davis/S.H. Davies and Flt Lts J.B.Abell/B.C.Whorwood) were scrambled
from *Tramp* to support the minesweeper HMS *Gavinton* (M1140) which was being
harassed by two Indonesian gunboats eight miles west of Singapore. Although the
first Javelin arrived on scene quickly, the gunboats had already disappeared.

The Confrontation officially ended on 11 August 1966 and the last operational
Javelin flight was flown on 16 August. The end of operations heralded a swift
reduction in the size of the Javelin squadrons in Singapore. At the height of the
Confrontation, 60 Squadron had been the largest Javelin squadron in the RAF
with a complement of over thirty aircraft, but in August both of the squadrons at
Tengah were reduced to an establishment of twelve aircraft and sixteen aircrew.
Operation *Tramp* continued, although at a much reduced readiness state. From
September, one aircraft was held at fifteen minutes, a commitment that was shared
in turns by both units. In early 1967, the *Tramp* state was reduced further to an
unarmed aircraft.

A four-ship formation of Javelin FAW 9Rs from 64 Squadron performing a flat turn over Singapore Island on 13 April 1967. (IWM)

Back to Normality

Without the distractions of operational flying and standby, the normal routine of the Javelin squadrons returned. PIs, controlled by the GCI site at Bukit Gombak, became the staple once more, and air combat and air-to-air gunnery were added when the opportunity presented itself. Visiting aircraft both from the RAF and passing RN carriers also added to the variety.

The end of the Confrontation and return to normality, 'brought a bit of a wake-up call' recalled Wg Cdr Miller. He continues: 'For the past four years… from the re-equipment with Javelins starting in July 1961… 60 Squadron had enjoyed the luxury of having almost one-hundred percent strength of experienced night-fighter crews [second and third tour pilots and navigators]. Now fresh young crews straight out of the newly re-opened night fighter OCU at Leuchars began to arrive with the news that soon the squadron would be fifty percent first tourists. A structured training programme was hastily put in place to bring these newcomers up to full operational status as soon as possible. One of the reasons was that, despite the declining threat

A formation of Javelin FAW 9s from 60 Squadron, led by Wg Cdr Fraser, set up for a flypast at Paya Lebar in December 1965. (J. Abell)

Javelins of 60 Squadron from RAF Kuching flying a routine patrol over Sarawak. (J. Abell)

Javelin FAW 9 (XH725) 'P' of 60 Squadron from RAF Tengah flying at low-level over the Malacca Straits. (J. Abell)

of cross-border intruders or night-time parachutists over Malaya, the squadron of Indonesian P-51 Mustangs based on an island barely fifty miles south of Singapore remained an ever-present threat. Even a single such raider at night dropping two five hundred pound bombs amidst the bright lights of the city could have had political/ international implications far beyond any physical damage or casualties. All crews had to maintain the ability to cope with these potential high-speed low-level targets at night (flying at three hundred and fifty knots-plus at heights down to fifty or a hundred feet) – a challenging task, even for a Firestreak-armed Javelin... Regardless of the new handling restrictions and the reduced squadron aircraft establishment (both aircraft and manpower), operational training continued unabated, with *Adexes* and APCs flown from both Tengah and Butterworth, small detachments or four aircraft returning there on a fairly regular basis to exercise the GCI controllers and the air-firing ranges in the Penang area. These operations [known as *Gas Iron*] continued through to late March 1968.'

Formations and Disbandment

On 30 April 1966, 60 Squadron also mounted a 'Diamond Sixteen' formation as part of their 50th Anniversary celebrations. Subsequently, Wg Cdr Miller instigated a tradition of flying large formations around the island at the end of each month, as a celebration – and a visible manifestation to all on the island of his groundcrew's hard work in achieving the monthly flying task.

On 64 Squadron, the groundcrew was also worked hard; Junior Tech T. Evans remembered: 'The weather ranged from cool and breezy to hot, sticky and humid

Javelin FAW 9 (XH725) 'P' becomes airborne for a routine training sortie from RAF Tengah. (J. Abell)

and of course wet. We generally got used to it but the aircraft did not. The humidity played havoc with the avionics. A very common entry in the Form 700 after a sortie was AI [radar] unserviceable – real pain for the radar and radio guys. When the weather was hot the Coke machine became a medicine cabinet and twenty-cent pieces for the machine became a rarity. Strange things happened when it rained. I saw four guys go out to strap in and dispatch two aircraft which were separated by only one aircraft. On the walk out it started to rain heavily. When the four guys returned to the line office two were soaking wet and two were bone dry. When it rained the line chief would bawl out "close those bloody hoods"… and we ALL got wet. But there was little point in running as one would get to maximum wetness in a very short time. Generally speaking the weather was not disruptive or uncomfortable from a working aspect. The line offices and the hangar offices were air conditioned, so this offered some respite at times. For the first few months it was hard to come to terms with Singapore daylight hours. At four o'clock it would be bright sunshine and I would start thinking, in UK terms, of a nice long balmy evening and perhaps a swim at the Britannia Club. Of course this never happened as by six o'clock it was dark.'

In March 1967, the Javelin force participated in large naval exercise *Fotex* 67, for which 64 Squadron was detached to Butterworth to defend the base against FAA Sea Vixens and Buccaneers operating at high speed and low level. Initially, 60 Squadron remained at Tengah, operating with the intercept controllers on HMS *Victorious*, but after the first three days of the exercise, eight Javelins of 60 Squadron flew to Kuala Lumpur. Here they flew air-combat patrols over convoys sailing through the Straits of Malacca.

Two months later, the Singapore *Adex* was the last exercise 64 Squadron was involved in before its disbandment. On 8 June, the Lightnings of 74 Squadron arrived to take the

A Javelin FAW 9R from 64 Squadron begins its take-off role at RAF Tengah. (G.R. Pitchfork)

place of 64 Squadron at Tengah. Wg Cdr Miller had intended to intercept the formation of Lightnings as it approached Singapore airspace, but an unfortunate underestimation of their speed by the GCI controller at Buket Gombak caused the Javelins to be scrambled too late. Two days later, a nineteen Javelin 'Round the Island' flypast was mounted in honour of the Queen's Birthday. Since this would be the last major sortie by the Javelins of 64 Squadron, the commanding officer (a navigator) was determined to lead it. However, the commanding officer of 60 Squadron (a pilot) was equally determined to do so and an amicable compromise was reached by both flying in the lead Javelin of a formation, which comprised a large 'Vee' of 64 Squadron aircraft and a diamond of 60 Squadron aircraft. On 15 June, 64 Squadron was disbanded, leaving 60 Squadron as the last Javelin squadron in RAF service. The Javelin FAW 9Rs of 64 Squadron were transferred to 60 Squadron and rapidly repainted with colours of their new unit.

Exercise *Gas Iron*

By mid-1967, Operation *Tramp* had been renamed, perhaps appropriately, Operation *Burden*. Scrambles were infrequent, but on 12 June Flt Lt Fletcher and Fg Off C.J. Donovan (FAW 9, XH846) were launched to intercept and shadow an TNI-AU Ilyushin Il-14 (reporting name Crate) transport as it flew along the international border in the middle of the Malacca Straits. Although the threat from Indonesia had now largely dissipated, growing communist-inspired unrest was causing some concern in Hong Kong. Headquarters FEAF therefore ordered 60 Squadron to provide a detachment of four aircraft to Hong Kong to provide a fighter presence, an exercise nicknamed '*Gas Iron*'.

Four Javelins led by Wg Cdr Miller left Singapore on 22 June, night-stopping at Labuan, before flying to RAF Kai Tak [Hong Kong] via Clarke Field, a USAF base in the Philippines. The last leg from Clarke was some 600 nautical miles over sea and with no diversions available at Hong Kong the Javelins were committed to landing there

Wg Cdr M.H. Miller, commanding officer of 60 Squadron, briefs the team in the crew room for the 'Diamond-Sixteen' formation to be flown in commemoration of the squadron's 50th Anniversary.
(M.H. Miller.)

The view along the flight line for 60 Squadron as crews strap in ready for the 50th Anniversary flypast; nearest the camera is the squadron's Javelin T3 (XH390).
(M.H. Miller)

An airborne view of the large formation as it closes up. (J. Abell)

The immaculate 'Diamond Sixteen' for the 50th Anniversary as seen from the ground at RAF Tengah on 31 April 1966. (G.R. Pitchfork)

The 64 Squadron hangar is a hive of activity as engineers carry out rectification work on Javelin FAW 9R (XH834). (T. Evans)

Groundcrew on 64 Squadron carry out a turnaround servicing on a Javelin FAW 9R (XH893). (T. Evans)

Javelin FAW 9 (XH777) 'R' of 60 Squadron flying at low level over the mangrove swamps. (P.J.J. Day)

Wg Cdr M.H. Miller, commanding officer 60 Squadron, and Wg Cdr B.E. de Iongh commanding officer 64 Squadron, lead the flypast for HM Queen Elizabeth's birthday over Singapore on 10 June 1967; it was also a farewell for 64 Squadron which disbanded a week later. The 'vee' of ten aircraft is from 64 Squadron and the 'Diamond Nine' from 60 Squadron. (C.J. Donovan)

Exercise 'Gas Iron' *– One: Two Javelin FAW 9Rs of 60 Squadron on the ramp at RAF Kai Tak, Hong Kong.* (M.H. Miller)

Exercise 'Gas Iron' *– Two: A pair of Javelin FAW 9Rs from 60 Squadron get airborne from RAF Kai Tak, against the backdrop of shipping in Hong Kong harbour.* (M.H. Miller)

Exercise 'Gas Iron' – Three: Night-time view of a Javelin FAW 9R (XH793) 'J' from 60 Squadron at RAF Kai Tak, backlit by the lights of Hong Kong island. (C.J. Donovan)

Exercise 'Gas Iron' – 4: a pair of 60 Squadron Javelin FAW 9Rs on the approach to Kai Tak, an approach which famously involved flying in amongst the flats of urban Kowloon (K.E. Fitchew)

once they had passed the halfway stage. A Canberra was therefore dispatched from Kai Tak to make radio contact with the Javelin formation as it approached the halfway mark to advise them of the latest weather in Hong Kong, so that they could decide whether to continue or return to the Philippines. The deployment went smoothly and the Javelins stayed in Hong Kong for a week.

There were two more deployments to Hong Kong: *Gas Iron II* took place from 11 July to 15 August and *Gas Iron III* followed in the first three weeks of November. These longer detachments provided an opportunity to swap personnel around halfway through, giving most of the crews the chance to enjoy the delights of Hong Kong.

The only fatal accident with a 60 Squadron Javelin occurred on 11 October. Fg Offs G.C. Barnard and H.J.C. Geeve were killed when their Javelin (FAW 9, XH788) broke up, possibly as a result of being overstressed in a hard turn. Two landing accidents in February were not fatal, but Wg Cdr Miller explained that, 'when two aircraft were eventually struck off charge as Cat.5 (beyond economical repair) scrap there was concern that the squadron might not have enough available to be sure of flying a Diamond Nine (by now something of a 60 'trademark') at its disbandment parade. A small recovery team (one Flt Sgt [Engines], a Cpl [Electronics] and a Fitter [Airframe]) was tasked to search the compound in a remote part of the airfield where Mk 9s 'retired' from 60 Squadron had been 'stored' (parked in the open) since June 1967, when the Mk 9Rs of 64 Squadron had replaced them. The team was told to select the best aircraft

Numbers 8 and 9 of a 60 Squadron formation on short finals to RAF Tengah...

All nine aircraft taxi back, offset in close order, past the Lightning F6s of 74 Squadron...

... while Number 7 touches down on the runway threshold.

... before finally turning into the 60 Squadron dispersal.
(All C.J. Donovan)

Javelin aircrews of 60 Squadron assemble for a last photograph at RAF Tengah in May 1968. (M.H. Miller)

there and get it serviceable to fly within a month. On 22 March 1968, a beaming Flt Sgt Pentland reported to the commanding officer "XH839 is ready to go, sir." "Well done, Flight, get yourself some flying kit and we'll give it a thorough air test," was the reply. A look of apprehension replaced the beam, but all was well... indeed, XH839 was the lead aircraft in Sixty's Diamond Nine Round the island.'

After two detachments to Butterworth in January and March for exercise *Tiger Rag*, a combined *Adex* and APC, and a night MPC in February, during which six Firestreaks were fired, the days of 60 Squadron as a Javelin unit came to a close. Characteristically, Wg Cdr Miller chose a uniquely striking format for the disbandment ceremony on 30 April 1968, describing how, 'in recognition of the squadron's role as a night/all-weather squadron, the period of the ceremony would embrace broad daylight, continue through the short period of twilight characteristic of the tropics, into full darkness.' The parade, which was held on the dispersal pan, included two flypasts – one in daylight by the squadron's now traditional 'Diamond Nine' led by Sqn Ldr J. Carter and Flt Lt Derbyshire, and then a fourship, led by Flt Lt K.E. Fitchew in darkness. The fourship in the dark was both visible and spectacular because it was flown in reheat. Despite the fixed power of the reheat, this latter configuration was possible thanks to the variable speed brake on the Javelin: Fitchew selected reheat against half airbrake, enabling the others to select reheat and then also use the airbrake lever to control the relative speed.

As the parade marched clear of the dispersal, ten Javelins taxied back on and turned to face the saluting platform for a simultaneous shutdown of twenty Sapphire engines. In that moment, all the lights were doused, except for a single spotlight shining on the flagstaff, and the *Last Post* sounded as the RAF ensign was lowered. It was a fitting farewell to both 60 Squadron and to the Gloster Javelin.

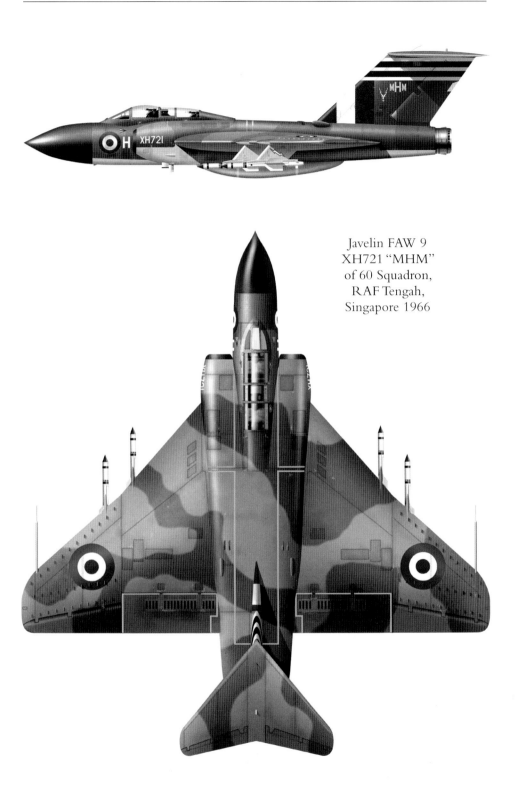

Javelin FAW 9
XH721 "MHM"
of 60 Squadron,
RAF Tengah,
Singapore 1966

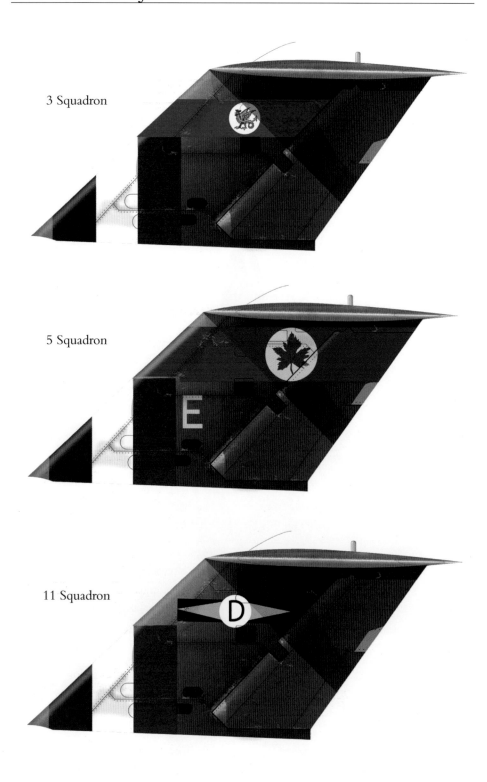

3 Squadron

5 Squadron

11 Squadron

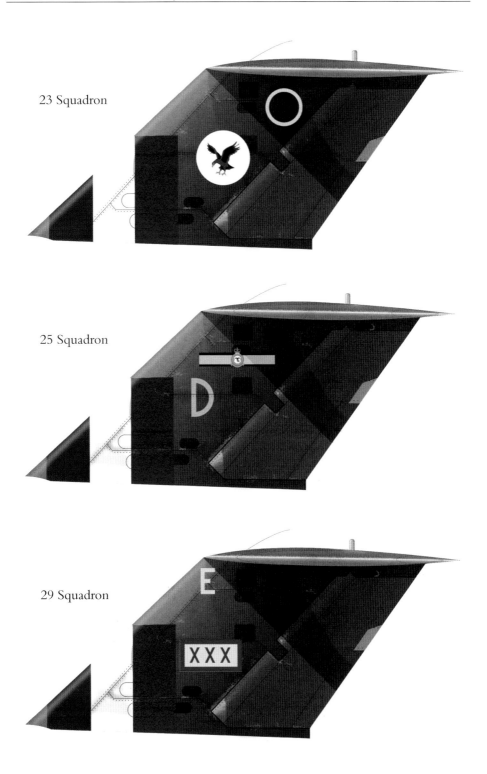

23 Squadron

25 Squadron

29 Squadron

33 Squadron

41 Squadron

46 Squadron

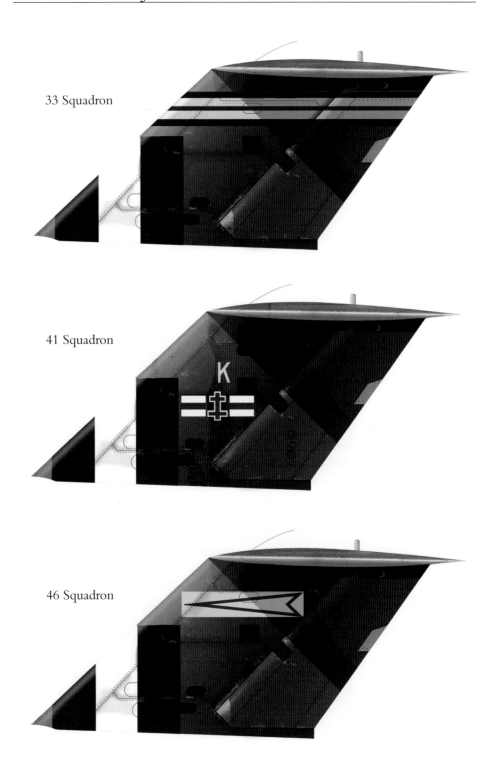

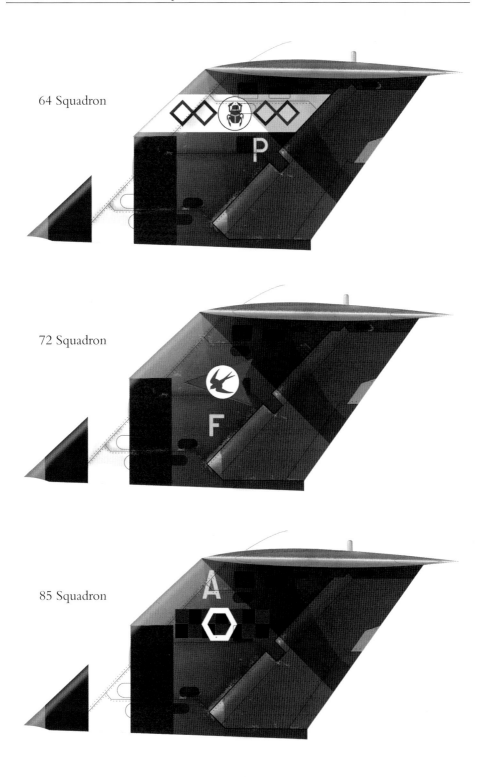

64 Squadron

72 Squadron

85 Squadron

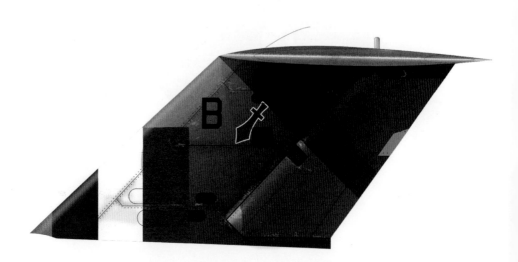

87 Squadron

89 Squadron

141 Squadron

151 Squadron

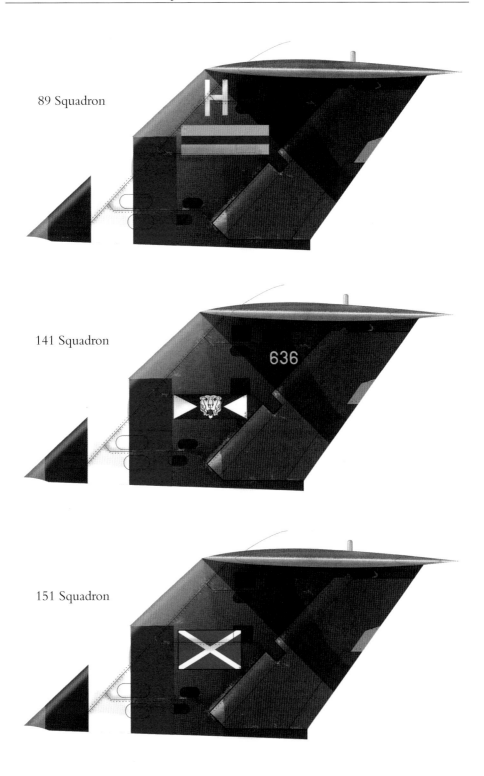

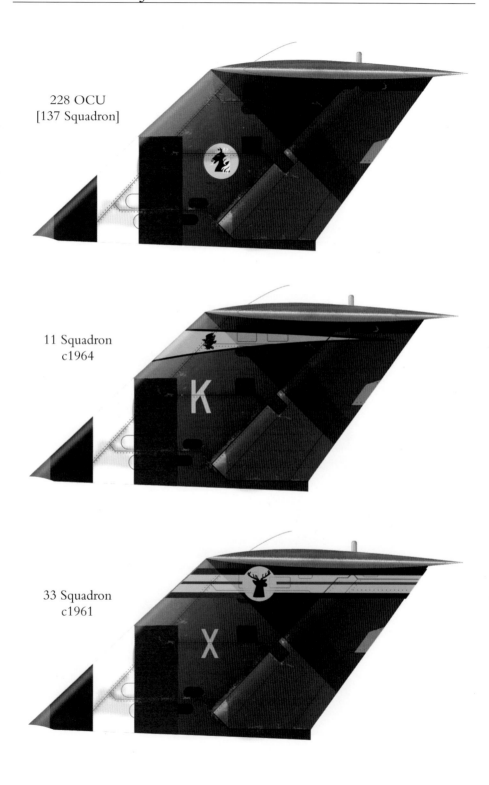

228 OCU
[137 Squadron]

11 Squadron
c1964

33 Squadron
c1961

Aircraft List

Research & Development (R&D), including trials work by Gloster Aircraft Company: Aircraft & Armaments Experimental Establishment (A&AEE): Royal Aircraft Establishment (RAE), Central Fighter Establishment (CFE).

Serial No	Mark	Unit	Date	Letter	Remarks
WD804	GA5 prototype	R&D			Crash-landed Boscombe Down, after losing elevators, 29 June 1952. Sqn Ldr W. A. Waterton, AFC - OK
WD808	GA5 prototype	R&D			Low-speed handling trial, crashed southwest of Bristol, 11 June 1953. Lt P. G. Lawrence, MBE, RN - killed
WT827	FAW 1 prototype	R&D			
WT830	FAW 1 prototype	R&D			
WT836	FAW 1 prototype	R&D			
WT841	T3 prototype	R&D			
XD158	FAW 2 prototype	R&D			
XA544	FAW 1	R&D			
XA545	FAW 1	R&D			
XA546	FAW 1	R&D/ RAE			Lost control during spinning trial - crashed Bristol Channel, 21 October 1954. Flt Lt R. J. Ross - killed
XA547	FAW 1	R&D CFE	1960	A	
XA548	FAW 1	R&D			
XA549	FAW 1	R&D 87 Sqn	1959	M	
XA550	FAW 1	R&D			
XA551	FAW 1	R&D			Became instructional airframe 7586M in 1958 (RAF Halton)
XA552	FAW 1	R&D			Development aircraft for DH Gyron Junior engine
XA553	FAW 1	R&D			
XA554	FAW 1	R&D 87 Sqn	3/56	B	Became instructional airframe 7662M in 1961 (RAF Halton)
XA555	FAW 1	R&D CFE	8/60	C	
XA556	FAW 1	R&D CFE	8/60		
XA557	FAW 1	R&D			
XA558	FAW 1	R&D 87 Sqn	3/58	A	Crashed after double engine failure, southeast of RAF Bruggen, 5 June 1958. Flt Lt J. E. Breakwell - killed, Fg Off J. J. Jackson, ejected - OK
XA559	FAW 1	R&D 87 Sqn	12/55 10/57	D	Engine exploded on start-up, RAF Bruggen, 22 July 1958. Flt Lt R. A. R. Carrey and Flt Lt A. Cooper - both OK
XA560	FAW 1	R&D	11/55		Development aircraft for Sapphire As.7 engine
XA561	FAW 1	R&D A&AEE	11/55		Lost control during spinning trial - crashed Isle of Wight, 8 December 1955. Sqn Ldr A. D. Dick, ejected - OK

Serial No	Mark	Unit	Date	Letter	Remarks
XA562	FAW 1	R&D	7/55		
XA563	FAW 1	R&D	11/55		
XA564	FAW 1	R&D	10/57		
XA565	FAW 1	CFE	1/56	A	
		46 Sqn	5/57	U	
		87 Sqn	11/57	K	
XA566	FAW 1	CFE	1/56	B	
		46 Sqn	5/57	N	
		87 Sqn	11/57	G	
XA567	FAW 1	R&D			
XA568	FAW 1	CFE	3/56	C	To College of Aeronautics
		46 Sqn	3/57	H	
XA569	FAW 1	46 Sqn	3/56	A	Un-commanded ejection of pilot at 41,000ft near
		87 Sqn	12/57	M	RAF Bruggen, 18 February 1959. Flt Lt R. A. R. Carrey, ejected – OK, Flt Lt A. Cooper – killed
XA570	FAW 1	46 Sqn	2/56	B	Crashed on GCA approach, RAF Odiham, 12 June 1956. Wg Cdr F. E. W. Birchfield, OBE, AFC and Fg Off B. Chambers – killed
XA571	FAW 1	46 Sqn	4/56	C	Became instructional airframe 7663M in 1961
		87 Sqn	1/58	O	(RAF Halton)
XA572	FAW 1	46 Sqn	3/56	D	
		87 Sqn	10/57	C	
XA618	FAW 1	46 Sqn	3/56	N	Severely damaged when starter motor
		87 Sqn	1959	B	disintegrated
XA619	FAW 1	46 Sqn	3/56	O	
		87 Sqn	11/57	H	
XA620	FAW 1	46 Sqn	4/56	E	Became instructional airframe 7723M in 1961
		87 Sqn	12/57		(RAF Cosford)
XA621	FAW 1	46 Sqn	4/56	F	
		87 Sqn	10/58	N	
XA622	FAW 1	46 Sqn	5/56	S	Instrument trials at RAE Farnborough
		R&D/	1958		
		RAE			
XA623	FAW 1	46 Sqn	5/56	G	
		87 Sqn	8/57	A	
		R&D	1959		
		AFDS	8/60	D	
XA624	FAW 1	46 Sqn	5/56	T	
		87 Sqn	11/57	J	
XA625	FAW 1	46 Sqn	3/56	P	Caught fire on start-up, RAF Bruggen, 12 May
		87 Sqn	12/57	L	1958. Flt Lt D. Allison and navigator – OK
XA626	FAW 1	46 Sqn	4/56	Q	
		87 Sqn	10/57	F	
XA627	FAW 1	46 Sqn	5/56	B	Became instructional airframe 7661M (RAF
		87 Sqn	10/57	E	St Athan)
XA628	FAW 1	46 Sqn	4/56	R	Became instructional airframe 7720M in 1959
		87 Sqn	8/57	B	(RAF St Athan)
XA629	FAW 4	R&D	9!/55		
		96 Sqn		H	
		3 Sqn	1/59	H	
XA630	FAW 4	R&D	10/56		
		96 Sqn	11/58	F	
		3 Sqn	1/59	A	
XA631	FAW 4	R&D	6/56		
		23 Sqn	4/58		
		72 Sqn	9/59	O	
		11 Sqn	12/59		
XA632	FAW 4	R&D	4/56		
		11 Sqn	7/59	A	

Serial No	Mark	Unit	Date	Letter	Remarks
XA633	FAW 4	R&D 96 Sqn 11 Sqn	5/56 12/58		
XA634	FAW 4	R&D	5/56		
XA635	FAW 4	96 Sqn 3 Sqn	11/58 1/59	L	
XA636	FAW 4	141 Sqn 41 Sqn 87 Sqn	9/57 7/58 11/59	636 E E	
XA637	FAW 4	141 Sqn 41 Sqn 11 Sqn	2/57 4/58	637 U J	
XA638	FAW 4	141 Sqn 96 Sqn 3 Sqn	3/57 10/58 1/59	J J	
XA639	FAW 4	141 Sqn 41 Sqn 87 Sqn	3/57 7/58 12/59	639 F F	
XA640	FAW 4	141 Sqn 41 Sqn 3 Sqn	3/57 7/58		Overran runway after hydraulic failure, RAF Geilenkirchen, 8 April 1960. Sqn Ldr C. P. Starck, Flt Lt J. G. Lomas - OK
XA641	FAW 5	5 Sqn	12/59	G	
XA642	FAW 5	AWDS	3/57		Double flameout, crashed off Skegness, 6 December 1957. Flt Lt A. Wright, Flt Lt R. Ashworth - both killed
XA643	FAW 5	CFE 228 OCU 11 Sqn	10/58 3/59	G Q	
XA644	FAW 4	R&D			Mid-air collision with Hunter F4 over Wootton-under-Edge, 24 August 1956. Mr E. B. Smith - killed, Flt Lt R. E. Jeffries, ejected - OK
XA645	FAW 5	87 Sqn 5 Sqn	9/58	M	Engine and fuselage fire, crashed near Wesel, 7 June 1962. Flt Lt J. H. M. Adam, Flt Lt C. M. H. Pinker, DFC - ejected safely
XA646	FAW 5	72 Sqn 228 OCU AWFLS	10/59 8/60 9/61	R C S	
XA647	FAW 5	151 Sqn 11 Sqn	3/57 9/61	B B	
XA648	FAW 5	CFE	3/57		Lost control during aerobatics, crashed near Fakenham, Norfolk, 20 September 1958. Sqn Ldr G. P. Kingston (solo) - ejected
XA649	FAW 5	R&D 5 Sqn	3/57 1959	D	
XA650	FAW 5	151 Sqn 11 Sqn	4/57 2/62	E C	
XA651	FAW 5	151 Sqn	5/57	D	
XA652	FAW 5	151 Sqn 228 OCU AWFLS	5/57 12/59 9/61	N,A T	
XA653	FAW 5	151 Sqn 228 OCU AWFLS		C S U	
XA654	FAW 5	23 Sqn 72 Sqn	4/58 6/59	J	
XA655	FAW 5	151 Sqn	9/58	F	
XA656	FAW 5	228 OCU AWFLS	5/57 9/61	L V	
XA657	FAW 5	CFE 23 Sqn 5 Sqn	10/58 4/59 1960	L	

Serial No	Mark	Unit	Date	Letter	Remarks
XA658	FAW 5	41 Sqn	11/58	E	
		5 Sqn	1960	E	
XA659	FAW 5	CFE	8/58		
		23 Sqn	9/59		
		5 Sqn	1960	F	
XA660	FAW 5	CFE	7/58		
		228 OCU	2/59	D	
		11 Sqn	2/62	A	
XA661	FAW 5	151 Sqn	12/57	Z	Caught fire on start-up, RAF Geilenkirchen, Germany, 29 October 1962. Flt Lt B Mason and navigator – OK
		11 Sqn	1961	F	
XA662	FAW 5	228 OCU	7/57	N	Double engine fire, crashed 30 miles west of RAF Leeming, 29 September 1959. Fg Off C. P. Cowper, Capt R. E. Nietz, USAF, both ejected – OK
XA663	FAW 5	228 OCU	8/57	P	
		CFE	5/58	Q	
		5 Sqn	2/62	K	
XA664	FAW 5	AWFLS	9/57	R	
		5 Sqn	9/61	P	
XA665	FAW 5	CFE	9/57	P	
		228 OCU	7/59		
		11 Sqn	1961	E	
XA666	FAW 5	228 OCU	7/57	G	
		41 Sqn	7/58		
		5 Sqn	1960	K	
XA667	FAW 5	228 OCU	8/57	O	
		41 Sqn	7/58	P	
		72 Sqn	3/60	P	
		228 OCU	8/60		
		11 Sqn	1961	L	
XA688	FAW 5	CFE	10/57	U	
		226 OCU	6/59	W	
		151 Sqn	8/61		
XA689	FAW 5	228 OCU	7/57	U	
		AWFLS	4/58	T	
		5 Sqn		C	
XA690	FAW 5	228 OCU	7/57	F	
		11 Sqn	1/62	M	
XA691	FAW 5	228 OCU	8/57	E	
		CFE	5/58	V	
		11 Sqn	2/62	P	
XA692	FAW 5	R&D			
		228 OCU	1961		
XA693	FAW 5	228 OCU	8/57	T	
XA694	FAW 5	228 OCU	8/57	R	
		151 Sqn	7/61	T	
		11 Sqn	3/62	K	
XA695	FAW 5	228 OCU	6/57	A	
		11 Sqn	8/61	J	
XA696	FAW 5	CFE	9/57	W	
		11 Sqn	9/61		
XA697	FAW 5	CFE	3/58	X	
		5 Sqn	8/61	O	
XA698	FAW 5	228 OCU	11/57	Y	
XA699	FAW 5	151 Sqn	5/57	F	
		5 Sqn	1959	C	
XA700	FAW 5	228 OCU	11/57	W	
		CFE	1961	R	
XA701	FAW 5	228 OCU	11/5	X	Caught fire on start-up, RAF West Raynham, 4 October 1962. Sqn Ldr G. K. Mossman and navigator – OK
		AWFCS	8/61	X	

Serial No	Mark	Unit	Date	Letter	Remarks
XA702	FAW 5	228 OCU	10/57	V	
		AWFL	8/61	Y	
XA703	FAW 5	228 OCU	9/57	I	
		41 Sqn	7/58	Y	
		72 Sqn	2/60	O	
		228 OCU	8/60		
		AWFLS	8/61	Z	
XA704	FAW 5	CFE	9/57		
		5 Sqn	1960	J	
XA705	FAW 5	CFE	9/57	Y	
		5 Sqn	8/61	N	
XA706	FAW 5	228 OCU	7/57	C	DBR – forced landing after electrical failure, RAF Leeming, 29 June 1960. Wg Cdr W. E. Thomas and navigator – OK
XA707	FAW 5	41 Sqn	8/58	A	
		5 Sqn	1960	B	
XA708	FAW 5	151 Sqn	6/57	U	
XA709	FAW 5	R&D	11/57		
		5 Sqn	1960	H	
XA710	FAW 5	151 Sqn	6/57	Y	
XA711	FAW 5	R&D			Used for gun firing trials
XA712	FAW 5	151 Sqn	5/57	S	
XA713	FAW 5	151 Sqn	6/57	W	
XA714	FAW 5	226 OCU	6/57	B	
		151 Sqn	8/61		
		11 Sqn	1961	O	
XA715	FAW 5	151 Sqn	6/57	T	
XA716	FAW 5	228 OCU	7/57	H	
		11 Sqn	1961	H	
XA717	FAW 5	151Sqn	6/57	V	
		11 Sqn	1961	N	
XA718	FAW 5	228 OCU	8/57	S	
		CFE	4/58	Z	
		5 Sqn	8/61	R	
XA719	FAW 5	228 OCU	7/57	J	
XA720	FAW 4	R&D	3/56		
		11 Sqn	12/59	B	
XA721	FAW 4	R&D	7/56		
		96 Sqn	9/58	E	
		3 Sqn	1/59	E	
XA722	FAW 4	23 Sqn	5/57		DBR – jet pipe failure, RAF Leconfield, 7 July 1959. Mst Plt A. F. Gundry and navigator – OK
		72 Sqn	7/59	N, M	
XA723	FAW 4	R&D	5/56		Cold weather trials, Canada
		11 Sqn	1960	H	
XA724	FAW 4	R&D			
		11 Sqn	1959	F	
XA725	FAW 4	R&D			
		11 Sqn	1960		
XA726	FAW 4	23 Sqn	5/57		
		72 Sqn	5/59	E	
XA727	FAW 4	23 Sqn	4/57		
		72 Sqn	5/59	G	
XA728	FAW 4	23 Sqn	5/57		
		72 Sqn	6/59	L	
XA729	FAW 4	23 Sqn	6/57		
		72 Sqn	4/59	A	
XA730	FAW 4	23 Sqn	5/57		
		72 Sqn	7/59	N	
		AWFCS	7/61		

Serial No	Mark	Unit	Date	Letter	Remarks
XA731	FAW 4	23 Sqn	5/57		
		72 Sq	7/59	M	
XA732	FAW 4	23 Sqn	5/57		Fuel tank caught fire while taxying, RAF Horsham St Faith, 25 May 1957. Flt Lt J. Wilkinson and navigator – OK
XA733	FAW 4	23 Sqn	4/57		
		72 Sqn	5/59	F	
		87 Sqn	1960	J	
XA734	FAW 4	23 Sqn	5/57		Engine fire, crashed near Wymondham Norfolk, 11 February 1958. Fg Off F. H. B. Stark, Fg Off P. Baigent, both ejected – OK
XA735	FAW 4	CFE	10/56	D	
		96 Sqn	1958	D	
		3 Sqn	1/59	D	
XA736	FAW 4	23 Sqn	5/57		
		72 Sqn	5/59	C	
XA737	FAW 4	23 Sqn	5/57		
		72 Sqn	6/59	K	
XA749	FAW 4	CFE	10/56	E	
		96 Sqn	10/58	C	
		3 Sqn	1/59	C	
XA750	FAW 4	141 Sqn	4/57		Lost control during low pass at Norvenich, 20 June 1959. Flt Lt W. S. Jacques and Fg Off D. A. Ritchie – both killed
		41 Sqn	7/58		
		96 Sqn	9/58	A	
		3 Sqn	1/59	A	
XA751	FAW 4	141 Sqn	4/57		Spun in from low-level aerobatics, RAF Wattsham, 11 July 1958. Capt E. Taylor, USAF – killed, Flt Lt B. K. Bedford, ejected – OK
		41 Sqn	5/58		
XA752	FAW 4	23 Sqn	5/57	F	Hit raised runway barrier on final approach to RAF Leeming, 2 March 1961. Flt Lt N. D. Want, Flt Lt Mitchell – OK
		72 Sqn	10/59	F	
XA753	FAW 4	23 Sqn			
		72 Sqn		B	
		AWFCS			
XA754	FAW 4	23 Sqn			Jet pipe split, hot gas leak, RAF Middleton St George, 27 October 1960. Flt Lt W. H. Olsen and navigator – OK
		72 Sqn		D	
XA755	FAW 4	23 Sqn			
		72 Sqn		H	
XA756	FAW 4	141 Sqn	3/57	756	
		41 Sqn	5/58	T	
		11 Sqn	5/60	C	
XA757	FAW 4	141 Sqn	3/57	757	
		41 Sqn	7/58	G	
		87 Sqn	12/59	K	
XA758	FAW 4	141 Sqn	3/57	758	
		41 Sqn	7/58	S	
		11 Sqn	2/60		
XA759	FAW 4	141 Sqn	3/57	759	
		41 Sqn	7/58	H	
		11 Sqn	2/60	L	
XA760	FAW 4	141 Sqn	3/57	760	
		41 Sqn	7/58	R	
		11 Sqn	1960	G	Written off by A&AEE on arrival because of its poor condition
		A&AEE	2/62		
XA761	FAW 4	141 Sqn	3/57	761	
		41 Sqn	7/58	J	
		87 Sqn	1/60	L	
XA762	FAW 4	141 Sqn	3/57	762	
		41 Sqn	4/58		
		96 Sqn	9/58	B	
		3 Sqn	1/59	B	

Serial No	Mark	Unit	Date	Letter	Remarks
XA763	FAW 4	CFE	10/56	F	
		96 Sqn	1/59	G	
		3 Sqn	1/59	G	
XA764	FAW 4	CFE	10/56	G	
		3 Sqn	4/59	M	
XA765	FAW 4	R&D	7/56		
		11 Sqn	1960	D	
XA766	FAW 4	141 Sqn	3/57	766	
		41 Sqn	7/58	Q	
		11 Sqn	2/60	M	
XA767	FAW 4	141 Sqn	3/57	767	
		41 Sqn	7/58	K	
		11 Sqn	1/60	E	
XA768	FAW 2	46 Sqn	3/58	D	
XA769	FAW 2	R&D			
XA770	FAW 2	R&D			
XA771	FAW 2	R&D			
XA772	FAW 2	46 Sqn	11/57	E	
XA773	FAW 2	46 Sqn	11/57	S	
XA774	FAW 2	89 Sqn	10/57	J	
		85 Sqn			
XA775	FAW 2	89 Sqn	11/57	N	
		85 Sqn			
XA776	FAW 2	46 Sqn	8/57	N	
XA777	FAW 2	46 Sqn	8/5	R	
XA778	FAW 2	R&D			Used by A&AEE as a calibration aircraft for Pressure Error Correction
XA779	FAW 2	89 Sqn	11/57	M	Stalled and spun in during low-speed pass, RAF Stradishall, 19 September 1958. Flt Lt D. H. Kenney and Fg Off G. R. Lewis - killed
XA780	FAW 2	46 Sqn	10/57	C	
XA781	FAW 2	89 Sqn	10/57	K	
		85 Sqn			
XA799	FAW 2	89 Sqn	11/57	Q	
		85 Sqn			
XA800	FAW 2	89 Sqn	10/57	L	DBR: undercarriage collapsed on landing, RAF Stradishall, 2 February 1958. Flt Lt B. R. Kent, Fg Off M. J. Fairey - OK
XA801	FAW 2	46 Sqn	8/57	F	
XA802	FAW 2	46 Sqn	8/57	D	Severely damaged in start-up fire, RAF Sylt, 17 March 1959. Flt Lt M. E. O. Haggerty, Flt Lt P. Fitzpatrick - OK
XA803	FAW 2	46 Sqn	8/57	H	DBR: undercarriage collapsed while towed, RAF Waterbeach, 24 April 1961
XA804	FAW 2	89 Sqn	3/58	R	
		85 Sqn			
XA805	FAW 2	46 Sqn	9/57	O, L	
XA806	FAW 2	89 Sqn	1/58	P	
		85 Sqn			
XA807	FAW 2	46 Sqn	8/57	P	
XA808	FAW 2	46 Sqn	5/58	V	
XA809	FAW 2	46 Sqn	1/58	T	
XA810	FAW 2	46 Sqn	7/57	G	
XA811	FAW 2	46 Sqn	10/57	A	
XA812	FAW 2	46 Sqn	9/57	B	
XA813	FAW 2	46 Sqn	9/57	U	DBR jet pipe failure, RAF Waterbeach, 12 April 1961.
XA814	FAW 2	46 Sqn			

Serial No	Mark	Unit	Date	Letter	Remarks
XA815	FAW 6	89 Sqn	10/57	E	
		85 Sqn	11/58		
XA816	FAW 6	89 Sqn	10/57	F	
		85 Sqn	11/58		
XA817	FAW 6	29 Sqn	12/57	E	
XA818	FAW 6	29 Sqn	11/57	B	
XA819	FAW 6	29 Sqn	3/58	V	
XA820	FAW 6	89 Sqn	9/57	C	
		85 Sqn	11/58		
XA821	FAW 6	R&D	4/57		
		29 Sqn	12/60	J	
XA822	FAW 6	29 Sqn	12/57	G	
XA823	FAW 6	29 Sqn	1/58	P	Collided with XA835 off Northumbrian coast, 21 May 1960. Flt Lt J. F. Wilson, Fg Off E. Wood, ejected – OK
XA824	FAW 6	29 Sqn	12/57	H	
XA825	FAW 6	29 Sqn	12/57	K	Hit ground in cloud, 4 miles northeast of Peebles, 21 November 1960. Flt Lt V. L. Hill and Flt Lt J. M. Knight – both killed
XA826	FAW 6	29 Sqn	3/58	S	
XA827	FAW 6	29 Sqn	2/58	R	
XA828	FAW 6	29 Sqn	3/58	U	
XA829	FAW 6	–			
XA830	FAW 6	46 Sqn	8/58	W	
		89 Sqn	10/58	W	
		85 Sqn			
XA831	FAW 6	R&D			
XA832	FAW 6	89 Sqn	4!/58	S	
		85 Sqn			
		AFDS	6/60		
XA833	FAW 6	–			
XA834	FAW 6	R&D			
XA835	FAW 6	29 Sqn	10/57	Z	Collided with XA823 off Northumbrian coast, 21 May 1960. Flt Lt D. J. Wyborn, Flt Lt D. S. J. Clark, ejected – OK
XA836	FAW 6	89 Sqn	9/57	B	
		85 Sqn		B	
		29 Sqn	6/60	P	
XH390	T 3	60 Sqn	10/61	T, O	
XH391	T 3	228 OCU	260	05	
XH392	T 3	228 OCU	3/59	04	
XH393	T 3	228 OCU	2/59	03	
		29 Sqn		V	
XH394	T 3	228 OCU	12/58	02	
		11 Sqn	8/61	X	
XH395	T 3	46 Sqn	1/59	Z	
		25 Sqn	8/61	Z	
		29 Sqn		W	
XH396	T 3	228 OCU	2/59	01	
		29 Sqn	8/61	D, Z	
XH397	T 3	41 Sqn	2/59		
		228 OCU	12/63	B	
XH432	T 3	23 Sqn	5/59	R, S	
XH433	T 3	29 Sqn	6/59	M	Caught fire on start-up, RAF Duxford, 3 Octber 1960
		CFE	2/60		
XH434	T 3	72 Sqn		T	
		64 Sqn	9/59	S	

Serial No	Mark	Unit	Date	Letter	Remarks
XH435	T 3	85 Sqn	7/59	Z	
		64 Sqn		S	
XH436	T 3	151 Sqn	6/59	R	Caught fire on start-up, RAF Leuchars, 14 May
		CFE/	9/61		1964. Wg Cdr W. J. Marriott (solo) - OK
		IRS			
XH437	T 3	33 Sqn	8/59	X	Caught fire on start-up, RAF Leuchars, 20
		23 Sqn			August 1964. Flt Lt E. P. Marsh, Sqn Ldr A.
					Coutts-Smith - OK
XH438	T 3	72 Sqn	8/59	T	
		CFE/	6/61		
		IRS			
XH443	T 3	25 Sqn	7/59	Z	
		AWFCS	1/60		
		CFE/	8/61	Z	
		IRS			
		29 Sqn			
XH444	T 3	3 Sqn	5/59		
		11 Sqn	1/66	Z	Ran off runway on landing (brake failure),
XH445	T 3	87 Sqn			RAF Tengah, 11 July 1966. Flt Lt J. R. J. Froud,
		60 Sqn		Q	Flt Lt K. W. Mills - OK
		64 Sqn		Z	
XH446	T 3	96 Sqn	5/59		
		3 Sqn			
		228 OCU	5/60	06	
		60 Sqn		Y	
		64 Sqn		Z	
		60 Sqn		Z	
XH447	T 3	5 Sqn	12/59	T	
XH687	FAW 5	151 Sqn	5/57	G	
XH688	FAW 5	151 Sqn	6/57	X	
		228 OCU	9/60	Q	
		5 Sqn	1961	D	
		11 Sqn		G	
XH689	FAW 5	151 Sqn	5/57		
		228 OCU	11/60	U	
		11 Sqn	1961	D	
XH690	FAW 5	151 Sqn	6/57	Z	
		5 Sqn	1959	A	
XH691	FAW 5	228 OCU	7/57	E	
XH692	FAW 5	228 OCU	8/57	K	Caught fire after landing, RAF Leeming, 4 May
					1961. Flt Lt A. P. Elphick and navigator - OK
XH693	FAW 6	89 Sqn	10/57	D	
		85 Sqn	11/58		
XH694	FAW 6	89 Sqn	10/57	A	
		85 Sqn	11/58	A	
XH695	FAW 6	89 Sqn	10/57	G	
		85 Sqn	11/58		
XH696	FAW 6	89 Sqn	10/57	H	
		85 Sqn	11/58		
XH697	FAW 6	29 Sqn	12/57	N	
XH698	FAW 6	29 Sqn	11/57	C	
XH699	FAW 6	29 Sqn	12/57	L	
XH700	FAW 6	29 Sqn	11/57	A	
XH701	FAW 6	29 Sqn	3/58	T	
XH702	FAW 6	46 Sqn	5/58	X	
		89 Sqn	10/58	X	
		85 Sqn	11/58		
		AFDS	5/60		
XH703	FAW 6	29 Sqn	6/60	Z	

Serial No	Mark	Unit	Date	Letter	Remarks
XH704	FAW 7	R&D			
	FAW 9R	23 Sqn	7/62	T	
XH705	FAW 7	R&D			
XH706	FAW 7	R&D			
XH707	FAW 7	R&D			
	FAW 9	23 Sqn	1960	T	
	FAW 9R	64 Sqn		F	
		60 Sqn		F, P	
XH708	FAW 7	R&D			Formation join up collided with XH896, crashed near RAF Tengah, 30 May 1967. Fg Off W. B. Kay and Cpl K. Ashbee – both killed
	FAW 9	64 Sqn	11/60	P	
XH709	FAW 9	64 Sqn	8/60	K	Controls seized, crashed north of Jahore, 14 June 1966. Fg Off E. J. Smith, Flt Lt L. A. Johnson, ejected – OK
XH710	FAW 7	R&D			Damaged in acid spill, Boscombe Down, 13 August 1961. Became instructional airframe 7748M (RAF Melksham)
XH711	FAW 7	R&D			
	FAW 9	29 Sqn		H	
XH712	FAW 7	R&D			
	FAW 9R	23 Sqn	10/62	V	
		29 Sqn	10/64	K	
XH713	FAW 7	R&D	7/57		Tropical trials
	FAW 9	33 Sqn		B	
		5 Sqn		B	
XH714	FAW 7	A&AEE	10/57		Un-commanded ejection of pilot, crashed near Kingston, Hants. 26 February 1958. Flt Lt R. S. May, Flt Lt J. V. Coates – both killed
XH715	FAW 7	33 Sqn	7/58	A	
	FAW 9	25 Sqn	1/62		
XH716	FAW 7	33 Sqn	7/58	C	
	FAW 9	25 Sqn	1/62	W	
XH717	FAW 7	64 Sqn	9/58	E	Caught fire on start-up, Butterworth, 26 April 1966. Flt Lt J. M. David and navigator – OK
	FAW 9	60 Sqn	6/61	C	
XH718	FAW 7	33 Sqn	9/58	X	
	FAW 9		1961		
XH719	FAW 9	33 Sqn	10/58	H	
		60 Sqn	6/61	B	
XH720	FAW 7	33 Sqn	9/58	G	Damaged on landing with port wheel brake locked, RAF Nicosia, 14 October 1959. Flt Lt J. S. C. Davies, Fg Off P. Miles – OK
XH721	FAW 7	33 Sqn	9/58	W	
	FAW 9	60 Sqn	8/61	H	
XH722	FAW 7	R&D	6/59		
	FAW 9	60 Sqn	6/61	F, P	
XH723	FAW 7	64 Sqn	12/58	O	Starboard engine exploded on take-off, burnt out, RAF Nicosia, 30 January 1964. Flt Lt R. B. Lloyd and Flt Lt F. M. Pearson – OK
		29 Sqn	5/61	R	
XH724	FAW 9	64 Sqn		N	Overran runway after brake failure, RAF Tengah, 3 April 1964. Flt Lt R. Aiken, Flt Lt E. Green – OK
		60 Sqn	8/61	F	
XH725	FAW 7	64 Sqn	11/58	F	
	FAW 9	29 Sqn	6/61	L	
		64 Sqn			
		60 Sqn		P	
XH746	FAW 7	R&D			
XH747	FAW 7	64 Sqn	9/57	B	Tail broke off during tail-chase, crashed near Singapore, 10 February 1964. Flt Lt G. L. Sykes, ejected – serious injury, Flt Lt T. P. Burns – ejected OK
	FAW 9	60 Sqn	6/61	B	

Serial No	Mark	Unit	Date	Letter	Remarks
XH748	FAW 7	CFE	3/58	G	
	FAW 9	33 Sqn	1/60		
XH749	FAW 7	CFE	4/58		Left runway on landing (starboard mainwheel
		64 Sqn	12/59	O	seized), RAF Butterworth, 17 November 1965.
	FAW 9	29 Sqn	5/61	G	Flt Lt B. C. Holland and navigator – OK
XH750	FAW 7	33 Sqn	7/58	R	Caught fire after engine failure 5 miles west of
					RAF Horsham St Faith, 9 July 1959. Flt Lt J. N.
					G. Buckley, Sgt D.V. Eke, ejected – OK
XH751	FAW 7	33 Sqn	7/58	S	
	FAW 9	60 Sqn	10/61	N	
XH752	FAW 7	64 Sqn	8/58	A	
	FAW 9	29 Sqn	5/61	S	
XH753	FAW 7	R&D	1/59		
	FAW 9				
XH754	FAW 7	R&D			Autopilot trials
XH755	FAW 7	CFE	6/58		Lost control and spun during air combat, east of
		23 Sqn	5/59	A	Tynemouth, 18 May 1962. Mst Plt J. E. Crowther
	FAW 9	33 Sqn	2/61	Y	ejected – OK, Mst Nav J. A. Farey, MBE – killed
XH756	FAW 7	CFE	6/58		
		23 Sqn	6/59	B	
	FAW 9	33 Sqn	1/61		
		5 Sqn	11/62	Z	
XH757	FAW 7	R&D	7/58		Tropical trials, Kano
	FAW 9	33 Sqn	9/60	F	
		5 Sqn	11/62	F	
XH758	FAW 7	CFE	6/58		Starboard engine exploded, 2 miles west of
		23 Sqn	8/59	C	Zonhoven, 17 October 1963. Flt Lt R. D. B.
	FAW 9	33 Sqn	3/61	R	Boulton, Flt Lt L. P. Morley – both ejected OK
		5 Sqn	11/62	R	
XH759	FAW 9R	R&D	9/60		Starter fire during servicing, RAF Tengah,
		64 Sqn		A	1 February 1968
		60 Sqn		A	
XH760	FAW 9	25 Sqn	12/59	B	
	FAW 9R	64 Sqn		E	
XH761	FAW 9	–			DBR – hydraulic failure on take-off, RAF Moreton
					Valence, 22 October 1959. Flt Lt R. Hanna – OK
XH762	FAW 9R	64 Sqn	7/60	F	
		29 Sqn		F	
XH763	FAW 9	23 Sqn	7/60	Q	
	FAW 9R	23 Sqn	10/62	Q	
		64 Sqn		C	
		60 Sqn		C	
XH764	FAW 9	64 Sqn	8/60		
	FAW 9R	29 Sqn		C	
XH765	FAW 9	64 Sqn	7/60		Ran off runway after abandoned take-off,
					Kalaikunda, India, 5 November 1963. Flt Lt R.
					J. Wark, Fg Off J. W. Jackson – OK
XH766	FAW 9R	64 Sqn	8/60	E	
		60 Sqn		E	
XH767	FAW 9	25 Sqn	12/59	A	
		11 Sqn	1/63	A	
XH768	FAW 9	64 Sqn	12/60	E	
XH769	FAW 9	25 Sqn	2/59	N	
		60 Sqn		C	
XH770	FAW 9	25 Sqn	1/60	K	
XH771	FAW 9	25 Sqn	7/60	F	
XH772	FAW 9	25 Sqn	1/60	G	

Serial No	Mark	Unit	Date	Letter	Remarks
XH773	FAW 9	33 Sqn	12/60	D	
		5 Sqn	11/62	D	
XH774	FAW 7	23 Sqn	7/59	D	Port engine exploded at start of take-off run,
	FAW 9	29 Sqn	4/61	B	RAF Akrotiri, 20 May 1964. Flt Lt R. B. Lloyd,
					Flt Lt F. M. Pearson - OK
XH775	FAW 7	23 Sqn	4/59	E	Night intercept - collided with XH781 and
					crashed near Brundall, 1 September 1959. Fg Off F.
					H. B. Stark, Fg Off P. Baigent, both ejected - OK
XH776	FAW 9	25 Sqn	11/60	P	DBR in servicing accident - Malta 1966
XH777	FAW 7	23 Sqn	8/59	F	Landed with port main wheel up RAF
	FAW 9	29 Sqn	4/61	N	Tengah, 5 February 1968. Flt Lt D. C. Bingham
		60 Sqn		R	navigator - OK
XH778	FAW 7	23 Sqn	5/59	G	Left runway (brake failure) undercarriage raised
	FAW 9	29 Sqn	3/61	C	to stop, RAF Akrotiri, 24 April 1964. Sqn Ldr
					M. G. Waudby and navigator - OK
XH779	FAW 7	23 Sqn	6/59	H	
	FAW 9	29 Sqn	4/61	U	
		60 Sqn	3/65	S	
XH780	FAW 9	33 Sqn		A	
		5 Sqn	11/62	A	
XH781	FAW 7	23 Sqn	4/59	J	Night intercept - collided with XH775: crashed
					near Brundall, 1 September 1959. Flt Lt C. S. T.
					C. Brooksbank, Sgt G. A. J. Spriggs - killed
XH782	FAW 7	GWTS	4/59	A	
	FAW 9	33 Sqn	1/61		
XH783	FAW 7	GWTS	3/59	B	
		23 Sqn		B	
XH784	FAW 7	GWTS	2/59	C	
		23 Sqn		C	
XH785	FAW 7	64 Sqn	9/58	C	Engine exploded 5 miles northwest of RAF
	FAW 9	60 Sqn	6/61	L	Tengah, 4 April 1966. Flt Lt E. C. Rawcliffe, Flt
					Lt A. Vosloo - ejected OK
XH786	FAW 7	33 Sqn	7/58	B	
	FAW 9		1961		
XH787	FAW 7	64 Sqn	9/58	R	Written off after port undercarriage leg would
	FAW 9	60 Sqn	6/61	G	not lower, RAF Butterworth, 5 April 1967. Fg
					Off F. C. Stephens, Flt Lt P. E. Dell - OK
XH788	FAW 7	64 Sqn	9/58	D	Disintegrated after overstress, RAF Tengah, 11
	FAW 9	60 Sqn	6/61	E	October 1967. Fg Off G. C. Barnard, Fg Off H.
					J. C. Geeve - both killed
XH789	FAW 7	64 Sqn	10/8	G	Overran runway after double hydraulic failure
					RAF Akrotiri, 31 July 1959. Flt Lt C. Grindley,
					Sgt S. Sanders - OK
XH790	FAW 7	AWDS	10/58		
		33 Sqn	8/59	R	
XH791	FAW 7	64 Sqn	1/59	P	Engine failure (centre-line closure) aircraft
	FAW 9	60 Sqn	7/61		broke up, Ganges delta, 5 August 1961. Flt Lt
					E. N. Owens, ejected - killed, Mst Nav A. D.
					Melton, ejected - OK
XH792	FAW 7	64 Sqn	11/59	G	
	FAW 9	29 Sqn	4/61	A	
		60 Sqn		U	
XH793	FAW 9	23 Sqn	4/60	A	
	FAW 9R	23 Sqn	11/62	A	
		64 Sqn		D	
		60 Sqn		J	
XH794	FAW 7	64 Sqn	10/58	L	Overran runway after hydraulic leak,
	FAW 9	33 Sqn	9/61	X	RAF Wildenrath, 9 March 1962. Sqn Ldr
					D. S. Burrows, Flt Sgt Christian - OK

Serial No	Mark	Unit	Date	Letter	Remarks
	FAW 7	33 Sqn	12/58	Y	
XH795	FAW 9				
XH833	FAW 7	33 Sqn	8/58	S	Starboard engine caught fire on take-off, RAF
	FAW 9	23 Sqn		I	Butterworth, 3 March 1965. Sqn Ldr J. G. Ince
		60 Sqn		F	and navigator - OK
XH834	FAW 7	64 Sqn	9/58	Z	
	FAW 9	29 Sqn	4/61	PDW	
	FAW 9R	64 Sqn		NP,	
XH835	FAW 7	33 Sqn	7/58	DH,	
	FAW 9	60 Sqn	7/61	K	
				D	
XH836	FAW 7	33 Sqn	7/58	O	Starboard engine exploded, crashed 75 miles
	FAW 9	60 Sqn	10/61		north of Singapore, 3 December 1962. Wg Cdr P.
				T	Smith, MBE, Sqn Ldr F. S. W. Jolliffe, ejected - OK
XH837	FAW 7	33 Sqn	8/58		
	FAW 9			F	
XH838	FAW 7	33 Sqn	8/58		Port undercarriage collapsed on landing, RAF
					Middleton St George, 20 September 1960.
				E	Capt J. C. Bailey, USAF and navigator - OK
XH839	FAW 7	33 Sqn	8/58	MHM,	
	FAW 9	60 Sqn	10/61	W	
				H	
XH840	FAW 7	64 Sqn	10/58		Starter explosion on engine start, RAF Luqa,
	FAW 9	60 Sqn	6/61	K	27 September 1961
XH841	FAW 7	64 Sqn	10/58	D	
	FAW 9	60 Sqn	6/61	J	
XH842	FAW 7	64 Sqn	10/58	A	
	FAW 9	60 Sqn	6/61		
XH843	FAW 9R	64 Sqn		T	Written off after starter explosion and fire,
		60 Sqn			RAF Tengah, 16 February 1968. Fg Off D.
				L	Binnie - OK
XH844	FAW 9	64 Sqn	11/61		Damaged by explosion on start-up, RAF
					Waterbeach, 13 April 1962. Flt Lt R. E.
				N	Lockhart, Flt Lt P. Hamilton - OK
XH845	FAW 9	23 Sqn	6/60	N	Port engine fire on take-off roll, RAF Leeming,
	FAW 9	23 Sqn	8/62		28 August 1964. Flt Lt M. R. Crosland and
				M	navigator - OK
XH846	FAW 7	64 Sqn	11/58	JF, J	
	FAW 9	60 Sqn	6/61	U	
XH847	FAW 9R	23 Sqn	8/62	G	Fractured undercarriage leg: left runway on
	FAW 9R	29 Sqn			landing RAF Khormaksar, 27 Jun 1966. Flt Lt
				B	W. A. Moxon, Fg Off H. Reid - OK
XH848	FAW 9R	23 Sqn	4/60	L	Hit slipstream in circuit, lost control, RAF
		29 Sqn			Akrotiri, 14 December 1966. Fg Off J. W.
				C	Pierce, Flt Lt T. P. Burns, ejected - OK
XH849	FAW 9	23 Sqn	5/60	C	
	FAW 9R	23 Sqn	9/62	H	
		29 Sqn		H	
		64 Sqn			
XH871	FAW 9	64 Sqn	8/60	M	
XH872	FAW 9R	64 Sqn	8/60	MHM	
		60 Sqn			
XH873	FAW 9	64 Sqn	8/60	A	
	FAW 9R	29 Sqn		A	
		23 Sqn	5/64		
XH874	FAW 9	64 Sqn	8/60		Caught fire during engine start, RAF Kuching,
				L	4 August 1964
XH875	FAW 9	64 Sqn	9/60		Caught fire during engine start, RAF Nicosia,
				N	27 May 1961
XH876	FAW 9	64 Sqn	9/60		Throttles jammed at idle, crashed Singapore,

Serial No	Mark	Unit	Date	Letter	Remarks
XH877	FAW 9R	64 Sqn	9/60	W	24 August 1966. Flt Lt P. J. Hart, Flt Lt J. J. Jackson, ejected – OK
XH878	FAW 9	64 Sqn	10/60	R	Port engine exploded after intercepting DC3, Tawau, Borneo, 22 June 1965. Flt Lt P. J. Hart, Flt Lt P. E. Dell, ejected – OK
XH879	FAW 9R	64 Sqn	11/60	D	Controls seized after hydraulic failure near Waterbeach, 27 November 1961. Sqn Ldr D. A. P. Saunders-Davies, Flt Lt P. R. Dougherty, ejected – OK
		60 Sqn		X	
XH880	FAW 9			JHW	
XH881	FAW 9	25 Sqn	2/60	M	
XH882	FAW 9	25 Sqn	4/60	L	
XH883	FAW 9	25 Sqn	3/60	H	
XH884	FAW 9	25 Sqn	3/60	C	
XH885	FAW 9	23 Sqn	5/60	E	DBR in servicing accident – Malta 1966
	FAW 9R	23 Sqn	7/62	E	
		64 Sqn	5/65	R	
XH886	FAW 9	23 Sqn	6/60	G	
	FAW 9R	23 Sqn	11/62	G	
		29 Sqn		J	
XH887	FAW 9	23 Sqn	6/60	F	Undercarriage did not lower, crashed off RAF Changi, 8 November 1965. Flt Lt K. E. Fitchew, Flt Lt A. Evans, both ejected – OK
	FAW 9R	64 Sqn		Q	
XH888	FAW 9	23 Sqn	6/60	K	
	FAW 9R	23 Sqn	10/62	K	
		29 Sqn	10/64	B	
XH889	FAW 9	23 Sqn	6/60	L, O	
	FAW 9R	23 Sqn	8/62	H	
		29 Sqn	10/64	M	
XH890	FAW 9	23 Sqn	6/60	M	Fractured undercarriage leg: left runway on landing Ndola, 2 June 1966. Flt Lt P. Morgan, Sqn Ldr A. G. L. Hutchinson – OK
	FAW 9R	23 Sqn	88/62	M	
		29 Sqn	10/64	H	
XH891	FAW 9	23 Sqn	6/60	H	
	FAW 9R	23 Sqn	8/62	H	
		29 Sqn		R	
XH892	FAW 9	23 Sqn	4/60	J	
	FAW 9R	23 Sqn	10/62	J	
		29 Sqn	10/64	B	
XH893	FAW 9	23 Sqn	5/60	D	
	FAW 9R	64 Sqn		V	
		60 Sqn		V	
XH894	FAW 9	23 Sqn	7/60	R	
	FAW 9R	23 Sqn	11/62	R	
		29 Sqn	10/64	E	
XH895	FAW 9	23 Sqn	8/60	P	
	FAW 9R	64 Sqn		G	
		60 Sqn		G	
XH896	FAW 9	64 Sqn	7/60	J	Formation join up hit by XH708, crashed near RAF Tengah, 30 May 1967. Fg Off P. McKellar, SAC M. Lokanadan, ejected – OK
	FAW 9R	60 Sqn		Y	
XH897	FAW 7	25 Sqn	3/59	M	
	FAW 9	33 Sqn	11/60	W	
		5 Sqn	11/62	W	
		R&D			Used by A&AEE as calibration aircraft for Pressure Error Correction
XH898	FAW 9R	25 Sqn	4/59	N	
	FAW 9	25 Sqn	12/60	D	
XH899	FAW 7			P	

Serial No	Mark	Unit	Date	Letter	Remarks
	FAW 9R	25 Sqn	4/59	D	
		29 Sqn		D	
XH900	FAW 7	23 Sqn	5/64	D	
		1 GWTS	3/59	D	
XH901	FAW 7	23 Sqn		E	
		1 GWTS	1/59	E	
XH902	FAW 7	23 Sqn		F	
	FAW 9	1 GWTS	2/59	F	
XH903	FAW 7	23 Sqn	4/62	K	
	FAW 9	23 Sqn	5/59	G	
		33 Sqn	3/61	G	
XH904	FAW 7	5 Sqn	11/62	L	
	FAW 9	23 Sqn	6/59	T	
		33 Sqn	6/61	T	
		5 Sqn	11/62	H	
XH905	FAW 7	29 Sqn		A	
	FAW 9	25 Sqn	11/58	E	
		33 Sqn	12/60	E	
XH906	FAW 7	5 Sqn		B	
	FAW 9	25 Sqn	12/58	Q	Collided with Canberra B2 during low-level PI, north of RAF Akrotiri, 26 October 1961. Flt Lt J. H. Morris - killed, Plt Off R. H. Lloyd, ejected - OK
		25 Sqn	12/60		
XH907	FAW 7			C	
	FAW 9	25 Sqn	12/58	C	
		33 Sqn	1/61	C	
XH908	FAW7	5 Sqn	11/62	D	
	FAW 9R	25 Sqn	1/59		
		64 Sqn		S	
XH909	FAW 7	60 Sqn		E	
	FAW 9	25 Sqn	12/58	R	Overstressed during emergency break (from RAF Leuchars), 20 October 1966. Flt Lt J H Adams - OK
		25 Sqn	12/60		
XH910	FAW 7	228 OCU		F	
	FAW 9	25 Sqn	12/58	L	
		29 Sqn	7/61	V	
XH911	FAW 7	60 Sqn		G	
	FAW 9	25 Sqn	2/59	J	
		33 Sqn	1/61	J	
XH912	FAW 7	5 Sqn	11/62	H	
	FAW 9	25 Sqn	2/59	S	
		33 Sqn	1/61	S	
XH955	FAW 7	5 Sqn	11/62	K	
		25 Sqn	4/59	J	
	FAW 9R	23 Sqn	1/60	T	Landed in undershoot, gear collapsed on landing at Labuan, 29 March 1964. Flt Lt P. J. Hart, Fl Lt K. C. Morgan - OK
XH956	FAW 7	60 Sqn		L	
		25 Sqn	2/59	E	
	FAW 9	23 Sqn	1/60		
		29 Sqn	4/65	W	
XH957	FAW 7	60 Sqn	2/61	J	
	FAW 9	25 Sqn	3/59	V	
		33 Sqn	1/61	V	
XH958	FAW 7	5 Sqn	11/62	M	
	FAW 9	23 Sqn	5/59	J	Landed with starboard wheel up, RAF Leuchars, 10 October 1966. Flt Lt G. E. Turner and navigator - OK
		29 Sqn	2/61		
		33 Sqn		Y	
		5 Sqn			
XH959	FAW 7	228 OCU	4/59	Q	
	FAW 9R	25 Sqn		U	Flew into the sea at night, off RAF Changi, 8 November 1965. Flt Lt P. J. Poppe - killed, Flt Lt B. G. W. Unsted - injured
		64 Sqn			
XH960	FAW 7		6/59	N	
	FAW 9	23 Sqn	3/61	V	
		29 Sqn		X	
XH961	FAW 9	60 Sqn		R	

Serial No	Mark	Unit	Date	Letter	Remarks
	FAW 9R	11 Sqn		C	Left runway on landing; hit storm ditch due
		29 Sqn		H	brake failure, 8 February 1968. Flt Lt K. E.
		64 Sqn		H	Fitchew, Flt Lt Holmes – OK
XH962	FAW 7	60 Sqn	5/59	O	
	FAW 9	23 Sqn	3/61	C	Left runway during formation take-off, RAF
		29 Sqn			Nicosia, 27 June 1963. Flt Lt J. R. J. Froud and
XH963	FAW 7		6/59	P	navigator – OK
	FAW 9	23 Sqn	6/61	Y	
		29 Sqn	4/65		
		64 Sqn			
XH964	FAW 7		8/59	Q	
	FAW 9	23 Sqn	3/61		
		R&D		J	
		29 Sqn		T	
XH965	FAW 9	60 Sqn			
XH966	FAW 8	R&D	3/60		
		R&D		X	
XH967	FAW 8	41 Sqn	4/59		
		R&D	11/61	L	
XH968	FAW 8	41 Sqn	7/59		
		R&D		H	
		85 Sqn		P	
XH969	FAW 8	41 Sqn	9/59		
		R&D	11/61	J	
XH970	FAW 8	41 Sqn	10/59		
XH971	FAW 8	R&D	12/59	A	
		41 Sqn			Disintegrated during break into circuit, RAF
					Geilenkirchen, 29 August 1961. Flt Lt J. L.
XH972	FAW 8		12/59		Hatch, Flt Lt J. C. P. Northall – both killed
XH973	FAW 8	AFDS	12/59	B	
XH974	FAW 8	41 Sqn	12/59	C	
XH975	FAW 8	41 Sqn	10/59		
XH976	FAW 8	AWDS	11/59		
XH977	FAW 8	AWDS	12/59	D	
XH978	FAW 8	41 Sqn	11/59	E	
XH979	FAW 8	41 Sqn	12/59		
XH980	FAW 8	AFDS	12/59	F	
XH981	FAW 8	41 Sqn	12/59	G	
XH982	FAW 8	41 Sqn	12/59	H	
XH983	FAW 8	41 Sqn	12/59	S	
XH984	FAW 8	41 Sqn	12/59	T	
XH985	FAW 8	41 Sqn	1/60	U	
XH986	FAW 8	41 Sqn	3/60	V	
XH987	FAW 8	41 Sqn	2/60	W	
XH988	FAW 8	41 Sqn	2/60	X	
		41 Sqn			Crashed after electrical failure near Carlisle, 9
					March 1960. Flt Lt M. Gill and Sgt R. Lydall,
XH989	FAW 8		2/60	Y	both ejected – OK
XH990	FAW 8	41 Sqn	3/60	Z	Landed with starboard wheel up, RAF
		41 Sqn			Marham, 2 August 1963. Flt Lt P. H Philip and
					navigator– OK
XH991	FAW 8		3/60	Q	
XH992	FAW 8	85 Sqn	3/60	P	
XH993	FAW 8	85 Sqn	3/60	J	
		85 Sqn		W	
		41 Sqn			

Serial No	Mark	Unit	Date	Letter	Remarks
XJ113	FAW 8	41 Sqn	4/60	X	Engine exploded on take-off, aircraft burnt out, RAF Wattisham, 11 Sepember 1963. Wg Cdr B. H. Howard and navigator - OK
XJ114	FAW 8	85 Sqn	3/60	K	
XJ115	FAW 8	85 Sqn	3/60	R	
XJ116	FAW 8	85 Sqn	4/60	X	
XJ117	FAW 8	85 Sqn	4/60	S	
XJ118	FAW 8	85 Sqn	5/60	D	
XJ119	FAW 8	85 Sqn	5/60	A	
XJ120	FAW 8	85 Sqn	6/60	G	
XJ121	FAW 8	85 Sqn	5/60	F	
XJ122	FAW 8	85 Sqn	6/60	E	
XJ123	FAW 8	85 Sqn	5/60	B	
XJ124	FAW 8	85 Sqn	9/60	C	
XJ125	FAW 8	R&D	8/59		
XJ126	FAW 8	85 Sqn	6/60	W	
XJ127	FAW 8	41 Sqn	7/61	M	
XJ128	FAW 8	85 Sqn	8/60	H	
XJ129	FAW 8	41 Sqn	9/61	A	Caught fire on start-up, RAF West Raynham, 10 July 1962
XJ130	FAW 8	41 Sqn	2/62	R	
XJ165	FAW 8	41 Sqn	2/62	K	
XK577	T 3	R&D			
XM336	T 3	IRF 23 Sqn 228 OCU	1/60	B	Double engine failure, crashed at Jaujac, Ardéche, France, 5 November 1963. Flt Lt C.V. Holman, Flt Lt D. E. Berks, ejected - OK

Index

Note —personnel are listed with rank held at first entry in the text.